The Illusion of Deterrence: The Roosevelt Presidency and the Origins of the Pacific War

Studies in International Politics

Leonard Davis Institute for International Relations
The Hebrew University, Jerusalem

STUDIES IN INTERNATIONAL POLITICS
LEONARD DAVIS INSTITUTE FOR
INTERNATIONAL RELATIONS
THE HEBREW UNIVERSITY, JERUSALEM

The Illusion of Deterrence: The Roosevelt Presidency and the Origins of the Pacific War

Abraham Ben-Zvi

Westview Press • Boulder and London

Studies in International Politics, Leonard Davis Institute for International Relations, The Hebrew University, Jerusalem

This Westview softcover edition is printed on acid-free paper and bound in softcovers that carry the highest rating of the National Association of State Textbook Administrators, in consultation with the Association of American Publishers and the Book Manufacturers' Institute.

Copyright © 1987 by Westview Press, Inc.

Published in 1987 in the United States of America by Westview Press, Inc.; Frederick A. Praeger, Publisher: 5500 Central Avenue, Boulder, Colorado 80301

Library of Congress Catalog Card Number: 87-51154
ISBN: 0-8133-7491-X

Composition for this book was provided by the author.
This book was produced without formal editing by the publisher.

Printed and bound in the United States of America

∞ The paper used in this publication meets the requirements of the American National Standard for Permanence of Paper for Printed Library Materials Z39.48-1984.

6   5   4   3   2   1

In memory of
Moshe (Mona) Rosenbaum,
beloved father and
father-in-law

Contents

ONE

Introduction:
A Theoretical Framework

In recent years, the hypothesis that decision makers in foreign policy act "in accordance with their perception of reality and not in response to reality itself" (Brecher, 1972: 11–12) has repeatedly appeared in the vastly expanded literature on the role of perception in international relations. A common denominator in these studies is the notion that perception and cognition intervene between the individual decision maker and his objective environment and that, therefore, the decisions he makes about his environment are subjective (Boulding, 1959: 120–121; Holsti, 1962: 244–251, 1976: 18–54; 1982: 87; North, 1967: 114; Jervis, 1968: 455–457, 1976; Young, 1968: 28, 30; Stein and Brecher, 1976: 34–35; Hermann, 1978: 49–68; George, 1979a: 95–124; Hopple and Rossa, 1981: 73; Lebow, 1981: 103).

Similarly, it is generally recognized that in order to experience and cope with the intricate, ambiguous reality of the environment in which he must operate, the individual must form "simplified, structured beliefs about the nature of [his] world" (Holsti, 1976: 20). The beliefs that comprise these "cognitive maps" provide the individual with a more or less coherent way of organizing what would otherwise be a confusing array of signals picked up by his senses (Holsti, 1976: 20; Suedfeld and Tetlock, 1977: 172; Jervis, 1982–83: 25). According to Jervis (1968: 455–456), these beliefs "will have greater impact on an actor's interpretation of data, the greater the ambiguity of the data and the higher the degree of confidence with which the actor holds the theory."

1

The conclusion is that every foreign policy decision maker operates within the context of psychological predispositions which function as the screen through which external information filters and is assimilated. This implies a serious potential for misperception and distortion of incoming stimuli. Indeed, a number of theoretical studies (Bentley, 1954; Boulding, 1956; McClelland, 1962: 456–458; Holsti, 1967: 29; Jervis, 1968: 457–458, 1976: 143, 1982–83: 24; Young, 1968: 38; George, 1969; Rapoport, 1960: 190–191, 200; Snyder and Diesing, 1977: 310–314; Lebow, 1981: 103) illustrate that, in attempting to fit new data into pre-existing theories and convictions, decision makers might ignore, reinterpret, or reconstruct all pieces of information which do not initially conform. They might also, as Jervis (1968: 475–476) hypothesizes, "see other states as more hostile than they are," and "view the behavior of others as more centralized, disciplined and coordinated than it is."

Seeking to expose those recurrent perceptual predispositions which aggravate the gap between the "psychological environment" and the "operational environment," George and Smoke—in their comprehensive study of deterrence in American foreign policy (1974)—focus on the constraints which a particular political and cultural setting may impose upon the thinking of policy makers. According to their analysis of events such as the Berlin blockade of 1948 and the outbreak of the Korean War (1974: 132–134, 162–172), U.S. decision makers attributed to their adversary their own line of reasoning. Overlooking the fact that the opponent did not have to follow a similar train of thought, they failed to supersede the boundaries that separated them from the conceptual world of their rival.

In another study which is closely patterned on the premises of *Deterrence in American Foreign Policy,* George—using the "process tracing" approach in the context of the Berlin Crisis of 1961—demonstrates the special role which divergent, incompatible images of the opponent can play in information processing:

> A general image of one's opponent as fundamentally hostile (the "hard-line" school) encourages the actor to define situations of interaction with that opponent as posing dangers to the actor's side. Ambiguous situations are perceived as threatening or as posing latent crisis. Ambiguous information about an opponent's behavior or intentions is likely to be interpreted as evidence of hostility. Discrepant incoming information that chal-

lenges the existing image of him as fundamentally hostile is discounted or ignored. (1979a: 102)

During the years immediately following the Pacific War, two divergent interpretations of American-Japanese relations in the pre-Pearl Harbor era emerged. One of these, the "revisionist" line, argued that the Roosevelt administration deliberately pushed the United States into a war with Japan in the Pacific as a way of entering the war in Europe through the back door. The other line—praising the administration for being realistic, consistent, and prescient—maintained that American diplomacy sincerely attempted "to avert a conflagration" in the Pacific (Ben-Zvi, 1975: 228).

Thus, in reviewing the early postwar literature on the origins of the Pacific War, one cannot avoid juxtaposing revisionist works—which charge the Roosevelt administration with the "sinister design" of intentionally provoking Japan into attacking the United States (Morgenstern, 1947; Beard, 1948; Chamberlin, 1950; Sanborn, 1951; Tansill, 1952; Barnes, 1953)—and pro-administration works (Bemis, 1948; Morison, 1948: 91–97; Feis, 1950, 1956; Rauch, 1950; Perkins, 1954).

Today, more than thirty-five years after the publication of the first major revisionist work (Beard, 1948), this heated debate of the late forties and early fifties seems to have subsided somewhat. There were but two major attempts to revive the revisionist case during the sixties (Fehrenback, 1967; Kubek, 1965); and today, scholars agree that all revisionist writers failed to build a solid case for this position. This consensus is apparent in most of the current textbooks dealing with American-Japanese relations in 1940 and 1941 (Wellborn, 1960; Leopold, 1962; DeConde, 1963; Divine, 1965; Irish and Frank, 1975), which by and large accept Leopold's conclusion (1962: 591) that the Roosevelt administration did not intentionally "goad the enemy into firing the first shot." However, the concurrence of most analysts regarding the inadequacy (if not total bankruptcy) of the revisionist line of interpretation should by no means imply that all facets of this subject have been dealt with and are fully explained. Indeed, there has yet to appear a study of the *political* origins of the Pacific War that employs analytical concepts and tools in order to help establish a more comprehensive and multidimensional picture of U.S. policies toward Japan (Ben-Zvi, 1975: 229).[1]

As a step toward replacing some of the crude dichotomies and simplistic generalizations that abound in the literature about Pearl Harbor and its origins, this work suggests a twofold typology of American policy makers and administration officials involved in the decision-making processes regarding Japan in 1940 and 1941. These typologies categorize both the content and structure of the images of Japan which were integrated into the policy makers' respective belief systems and which, at times, influenced their specific policy lines.

The exploration of these patterns of perception and interpretation (combined with an analysis of the political bureaucratic factors and conditions which mediate between the "psychological environment" and the "operational environment" and can thus determine the extent to which certain perceptions could be channelized into action) is intended to clarify a number of hitherto unresolved and controversial questions concerning American-Japanese relations during the period preceding the Pearl Harbor attack. At the same time it is designed to shed light on at least some of the basic sources of human conduct in recurrent crisis situations.

Indeed, although the following analysis will be confined to the delimited context of the American-Japanese crisis as it unfolded in 1940 and 1941, this episode is viewed as a prism through which certain general, recurrent patterns of thinking and behavior can be observed. In other words, this examination of American images and policies is conceived as an illustration of "some larger phenomenon" (George, 1979b: 51) rather than of a single, unique event (which, as such, can only be explained in purely idiosyncratic and highly specific terms). It seeks to elucidate a wide complex of perceptual (as well as political and bureaucratic) mechanisms which are predicated upon certain inherent human propensities. Thus, treated as an instance of a wider type of undertaking that occurs repeatedly throughout history, the present case study can contribute to the development of a highly differentiated, multifaceted theory and to the formulation of certain generalizations and typologies. These might, in turn, serve as "indicators" of predictive value (Eckstein, 1975: 99; George, 1979b: 45, 50–51).

More specifically, it is hoped that by exposing the conceptual origins of the American failure to deter Japan, a higher level of understanding regarding the *general* limits of deterrence and of coercive diplomacy will be achieved. It is similarly hoped that by underscoring the role which certain basic cognitive (and bureaucratic) processes played in precipitating the Pacific War, this "disciplined-configurative" case study (Eckstein, 1975: 99) will help to sensitize many a political actor to the ever-present danger of misperceiving incoming information. Thus it may pave the way toward a clearer recognition of the difficulties stemming from a constant need to cope with a welter of ambiguous and often conflicting stimuli.

Viewed from this perspective, the analysis of the divergent images held by those constituting the Roosevelt policy elite on the eve of Pearl Harbor—to which we now turn—indeed bears a significance "far exceeding any tale of an isolated catastrophe that might have been the result of negligence or stupidity or treachery, however lurid" (Wohlstetter, 1962: 397).

NOTES

1. Wohlstetter (1962) gives a comprehensive picture of how information was gathered and interpreted by the U.S. intelligence community on the eve of Pearl Harbor.

TWO

The Policy Makers:
A Bureaucratic
Perspective

American policy toward Japan on the eve of the Pearl Harbor attack was not the product of a rational, value-maximizing decisional process. Rather, it constituted the cumulative, aggregate outcome of several "bargaining games" in which various individuals—who differed from one another in terms of their respective power, resolve, bargaining skill, and world view—strove to build a "majority coalition" (the terminology is from Snyder and Diesing, 1977: 349) which would enable them to carry out their preferred Pacific strategy. Thus, far from being "a calculated solution to a strategic problem" (Snyder and Diesing, 1977: 340), reached by a unitary actor on the basis of a scrupulous comparative assessment of the expected outcome of several well-defined, mutually exclusive policy alternatives (Steinbrunner, 1974: 25–46), the process by which the American posture in the Pacific was actually shaped and delineated was closely patterned on the premises of the "bureaucratic politics" theory. Developed by Allison (1971) and Halperin (1974), this conceptual approach views the formulation of foreign policy as a function of the continuous competition among various political actors, who are arranged hierarchically in the national decision-making unit, and who see "different faces of an issue" (Allison, 1971: 162). The general picture this theory gives of the decision-making process, then, is of partisan actors, "maneuvering into alliances and oppositions, each trying to capture the

7

commitment of the central decision maker" (Snyder and Diesing, 1977: 353), rather than of unity and cohesion in pursuit of a single homogeneous good.

In applying some of the premises of the bureaucratic politics theory to the context of American-Japanese relations in 1940 and 1941, we must pose a series of guideline questions. First, who were the individuals comprising Roosevelt's decision-making machinery and competing with one another in an attempt to shape American policy in the Pacific in accordance with their respective worldviews and images of Japan? Furthermore, what was the composition and nature of the "majority coalition" which managed to win most of the "bargaining games" during the period preceding the war? Finally, what contributed to this victory, which enabled the winning faction to carry out its advocated strategy and thus to translate into reality its preconceived visions of the world?

The subject of American-Japanese relations was not dealt with exclusively by individuals operating within separate departments (such as the U.S. State Department). Nor were all the participants in policy formulation continuously involved in the decision-making process. For example, Postmaster General Frank C. Walker and the two Roman Catholic clerics, Bishop James E. Walsh and Father James M. Drought, appeared only briefly in the foreground of the American-Japanese scene.[1] A number of prominent figures, however, were so involved.

Certain members of the State Department, headed by Cordell Hull, played a significant role in the formulation of U.S. policy toward Japan. In addition to his deep involvement in the negotiations with Japanese representatives (the Hull-Nomura conversations) which took place in Washington from February to November 1941, Hull contributed personally to the formulation of some of the most crucial decisions concerning Japan in 1941. Thus, notwithstanding "Roosevelt's penchant for bypassing the secretary of state" (De Santis, 1980: 203), Hull did manage to make a considerable impact on the course of American diplomacy in the Pacific theater on the eve of the war. Several other State Department officials, including Undersecretary Sumner Welles, political affairs advisor Stanley K. Hornbeck, the chief of the Far Eastern Division, Maxwell U. Hamilton, and his assistant, Joseph W. Ballantine, were also involved in the process by which American policy in the Pacific was shaped.

The State Department officials involved in this process were a heterogeneous group, whose leading members frequently clashed with each other on questions of basic strategy. Specifically, Hull, Welles, and Hamilton *initially* supported a cautious posture toward Japan (which, in the case of Welles, derived, at least partially, from his exposure to Japanese culture when he served in the American embassy in Tokyo from 1915 to 1917). In contrast Hornbeck consistently advocated, in 1940 and 1941, a "harsher line toward the Japanese" (De Santis, 1980: 52), and openly challenged the Department's predilection for a restrained course. Hornbeck, an experienced and highly respected regional expert, managed to forge an alliance with several prominent policy makers outside the State Department (as well as with such interest groups as the Price Committee for Non-Participation in Japanese Aggression), who shared his nonconciliatory approach toward Tokyo (Cohen, 1978: 221, 238). On a number of occasions, he went so far as to encourage Roger S. Greene of the Price Committee to issue statements criticizing official policy on the question of economic sanctions against Japan (Cohen, 1973: 450). On another occasion, in September 1941, Hornbeck urged Greene to appeal to Hull and Roosevelt not to conclude any agreement with Japan "that sacrificed American principles respecting China" (Cohen, 1973: 454). That relations between Hull and Welles were, in general, strained, further weakened this relatively moderate "blocking coalition" within the State Department in its attempt to contain the more assertive "opposing coalition" (Snyder and Diesing, 1977: 350).

Yet another factor which adversely affected Hull's bargaining position vis-à-vis several other administration officials was his health, which failed him repeatedly during the period preceding Pearl Harbor. On one occasion, for example, he was compelled to convalesce at White Sulphur Springs at the very moment that the issue of imposing economic sanctions upon Japan was debated in the cabinet. While Hull sent frequent messages from White Springs urging caution (Divine, 1965: 190), his absence from a number of crucial cabinet sessions left Undersecretary Welles (who advocated moderation but lacked Hull's prestige and standing in the cabinet) with the insurmountable task of confronting a cohesive, powerful group of decision makers who urged a punitive course of action in the Pacific. This no doubt contributed to the partial success of the hard-line coalition.

The American Embassy in Tokyo, headed by the experienced diplomat Joseph C. Grew (who continued to support an accommodative posture), was occasionally involved in policy consultations. However, Ambassador Grew's role in the shaping of the U.S. Far Eastern policy was, in general, limited, and it became even more so in the wake of Hull's decision, late in July 1941, to finally give support to the maximalist, intransigent "majority coalition." For example, in August and September 1941, Grew's repeated and emphatic pleas that the proposed Roosevelt-Konoye meeting take place were completely ignored by Hull. At the same time, the ambassador's freedom of action was circumscribed by the State Department, which provided him with very specific instructions leaving no room for any personal contribution. In November 1941, when negotiations with Japan had reached their final and most crucial phase, the embassy's contribution to the policy-making process reached its nadir. No attention whatsoever was paid to the views, analyses, evaluations, and recommendations expressed by Ambassador Grew and his staff. The embassy was not even provided with relevant information pertaining to the American-Japanese conversations, nor was it consulted as to the conduct of U.S. policy toward Japan (Heinrichs, 1966: 309).

Indeed, during the period immediately preceding Pearl Harbor, Grew remained—as he himself pointed out in his telegram of November 3, 1941 (Roosevelt, 1933–45, *President's Secretary's File* [hereafter PSF], Box 30)—"out of touch with the Administration's thoughts and intentions."

The State Department was not operating in a political or administrative vacuum. It had to cope with various pressures from within, as well as from influential individuals outside the department (such as Secretary of War Stimson and Secretary of the Treasury Morgenthau, who continuously insisted on a coercive posture toward Japan). It also had to accommodate itself to forces outside the administration, such as Congress and various pressure groups (and primarily the powerful Price Committee), and thus remain sensitive to the general mood of the public regarding Japan (Cohen, 1973: 438). In addition, the State Department was constantly confronted with a welter of considerations originating in the international arena. Some of these factors, such as Hitler's victory in France in the spring of 1940, were seemingly remote but nonetheless proved relevant to the course of Japanese-American relations. Others, such as the Tripartite Pact of September 27, 1940, constituted direct and immediate pressure that required the United States to either react or accommodate itself. Similarly, in late November 1941, explicit pressures were exerted upon the State Department by the Chinese government in an effort to prevent any sort of modus vivendi with Japan. In brief, then, internal and external pressures, certain deep-rooted preconceptions, and of course existing policy lines considerably constrained the State Department's freedom of choice in formulating American policies toward Japan.

Significant as the role played by the State Department was, other individuals within the War, Navy, and Treasury departments were also deeply involved in various aspects of relations between the United States and Japan. Secretary of War (from June 1940) Henry L. Stimson was intensely interested in the question of American-Japanese relations. Stimson held certain fixed views as to the policies the United States should pursue toward Japan—views that had apparently been shaped in the course of the "Manchurian crisis" of 1931, when he served as secretary of state in President Hoover's administration.

Stimson, a highly respected *Republican* senior statesman, was persuaded by Roosevelt to join the administration in an attempt to broaden the margin of public support for its increasingly interventionist posture in Europe. He was one of the most powerful members of the Roosevelt entourage. Stimson was fully aware of his unique bargaining position; the president was naturally most anxious not to alienate a prominent member of the opposition party, whose presence in a key position in his cabinet helped him gain legitimacy for his much-disputed policy of containing the Nazi menace in Europe. Thus Stimson was uninhibited in presenting the strategy he advocated during cabinet meetings and consultations with Hull, who had succeeded him as secretary of state in 1933, and with whom he retained a long-standing relationship of mutual respect. Stimson also met regularly with several other cabinet members (e.g., Frank Knox, secretary of the navy and Henry Morgenthau, Jr., secretary of the treasury), who constituted an informal "war council" which often dealt with foreign policy questions (Langer and Gleason, 1953: 693). In the hope of persuading the president to adopt strong coercive measures against Japan, Stimson, like Hornbeck, occasionally encouraged advocates of a nonconciliatory posture toward Japan, such as Harry Price and Roger Greene, to intensify their lobbying activity (Cohen, 1978: 229).

Within the army, a number of military planners, strategists, and intelligence officers also explored American-Japanese relations in numerous memoranda and intelligence reports related to the Far Eastern situation. Some of their purely military reports contained political implications (U.S. Congress, Pearl Harbor *Hearings*, 1946: Part 19, 1067, 1344–1347).

Henry Morgenthau, Jr., secretary of the treasury, was also deeply involved in the question of American-Japanese relations. As a close friend of President Roosevelt, Morgenthau was able to maintain a special status within the cabinet, and the president frequently gave much weight to his recommendations on economic and political issues. In general, Morgenthau demonstrated an abiding interest in political matters, with a particular bent for the field of foreign relations. His frequent forays into international political matters were sometimes made without the knowledge of the State Department. As Hull remarks (1948: Vol. 1, 209), "Morgenthau often interfered in foreign affairs, and sometimes took steps directly at variance with those of the State Department." Morgenthau's personal relations with the president were very close, and he occasionally "induced the President to grant him jurisdiction which infringed on that of the State, War or Navy Departments" (Gardner, 1973: 281).

Like Stimson, with whom he forged a powerful majority alliance, Morgenthau held well-established views regarding American-Japanese relations. His vigorous advocacy of these opinions frequently brought him to the point of open conflict with the State Department, and principally with Sumner Welles. For example, in several cabinet discussions Morgenthau vehemently supported the idea of imposing economic sanctions upon Japan (Blum, 1970: 388, 391, 394, 396).

In seeking to influence the president's views and thus "to capture the central decision maker for his coalition" (Snyder and Diesing, 1977: 352), Morgenthau—using the same technique employed consistently by Secretary Knox (see, e.g., his letter of January 23, 1940, in PSF, Box 82, Frank Knox)—systematically forwarded to Roosevelt carefully selected information coinciding with the policies he was urging. This material included excerpts from newspapers, intelligence reports, messages, and memoranda received from various American governors, senators, scholars, newspapermen, and other public figures. For example, on June 18, 1939, Morgenthau sent Roosevelt a *New York Times* article of the previous day which stated that the only effective policy toward Japan was one based on "retaliatory measures": "Almost every act of Japan's policy since 1931 has been opposed by a Western power intrinsically stronger than Japan, but none has carried its opposition beyond diplomatic protests," the article explained. As a result, the article concluded, Japan had become "filled with self-confidence and intoxicated," believing, in the light of past experiences, that the United States would never "participate in retaliatory measures" against her. Similarly, on December 30, 1940, Morgenthau delivered to Roosevelt a copy of an article published in the *New Republic* that strongly criticized "the American appeasement circle" (Roosevelt, 1933–45, *President's Personal File* [hereafter PPF], 1940: Box 82, Treasury Department, Henry Morgenthau, Jr.).

Throughout the second half of 1941, Morgenthau sent Roosevelt copies of a weekly survey called "Editorial Opinion: Reports on Questions of Foreign Affairs," prepared by the Treasury Department and consisting of selective reviews of the American press regarding current international issues. On several occasions the selection of data and its interpretation somewhat distorted the extent of hostility in the American press toward Japan (PPF, 1940: Box 83, Treasury Department, Henry Morgenthau, Jr.).

Morgenthau can be thought of as a powerful partisan coalition builder in a highly complex bureaucratic game. On occasion he used his administrative powers to implement his preferred strategy de facto (the de facto oil embargo which the Treasury Department was most instrumental in imposing upon Japan in 1941 clearly illustrates this pattern). He also consistently tried to use access to the president as a stepping stone for "pressing his case, by presenting selected information, urging selected values, and offering slanted interpretations and arguments" (Snyder and Diesing, 1977: 352). In addition to the various forms of direct pressure used by Morgenthau in his effort to shape U.S. Far Eastern diplomacy in accordance with his preconceptions, he resorted on occasion to more subtle tactics. For example, exploiting to the full his position at the White House, he was instrumental in arranging several meetings between such strong advocates of a harsh policy toward Japan as the Chinese ambassador to Washington, T. V. Soong, and President Roosevelt (PPF Box 2907).

And indeed, the secretary of the treasury ultimately managed to gain the full support of Roosevelt, who was initially skeptical of his hard-line posture toward Japan (Blum, 1970: 396). As Kubek (1965: 17) notes, in November 1941, the Treasury Department played "an increasingly formative role in the development of American Far Eastern policy."

Most significant in this context was the far-reaching memorandum entitled "An Approach to the Problem of Eliminating Tension with Japan and Helping Defeat of Germany" which was drafted by Harry Drexler White, director of monetary research in the Treasury Department. It was sent by Morgenthau to Roosevelt and Hull on November 18, 1941 (PSF, 1941: Box 60; Japan: October-December), and provided the infrastructure for Hull's "Ten Point Plan." This maximalistic document, which incorporated many of the provisions of the White memorandum, was submitted to the Japanese negotiators in Washington on November 26, 1941, and sealed the fate of the prolonged diplomatic effort to reach an understanding on at least some of the outstanding issues separating the two countries. At a group meeting on November 22, 1941, Morgenthau, who was not modest about his role in shaping U.S. Far Eastern policy at that crucial juncture (*The Morgenthau Diary*, 1941: Book 464, November 22–24), noted, "He [White] had done a very amazing memorandum of suggestions on the Japanese questions, and I sent them over to the President and Mr. Hull, so I asked the President whether he had been able to make any use of them . . . and he said yes, they had incorporated several of [these] suggestions."

Another policy maker demonstrating a constant interest in American-Japanese relations was Secretary of the Interior Harold L. Ickes, a liberal New Dealer whose views in some ways resembled those of Stimson and Morgenthau. Prior to June 1941, Ickes's direct contribution to the formulation of U.S. policy toward Japan was very limited. However, following his appointment on May 28, 1941, as petroleum coordinator for national defense, Ickes's influence increased considerably, and he was capable of intervening more forcefully in the debate on the imposition of a total oil embargo on Japan.

Ickes was not always successful in wielding his administrative and bargaining power to achieve the economic-political goals he desired. On June 20, 1941, for example, he passed on to Roosevelt a cable received on June 17 from Edwin W. Pauley, petroleum coordinator for war in Europe, which suggested "military action to prevent Japan from expanding into the Netherlands East Indies" (Roosevelt, 1933–45, *Papers as President: President's Official File* [hereafter POF], 1941–1945; Box 4, Japan). On that occasion, the president was neither persuaded nor impressed by Ickes's argument.

As for the White House staff's contribution to the formulation of U.S. policy toward Japan, three presidential advisors (Norman H. Davies, Harry Hopkins, and Lauchlin Currie) were occasionally involved in questions pertaining to American-Japanese relations. All participated in meetings and consultations with the president and cabinet members, although none assisted in formulating any of the most crucial decisions made by the Roosevelt administration during 1940 and 1941.

An examination of President Roosevelt's actions up to the very eve of Pearl Harbor indicates clearly that he was primarily interested in Europe and was concerned with the Far East only insofar as it affected the European war. Indeed, because of his preoccupation with Europe, President Roosevelt did not play a leading role in formulating U.S. policy toward Japan. Even on those infrequent occasions when the president did initiate a significant course of action (such as his formula for an

American-Japanese modus vivendi), he did not insist that his original recommendations be carried out and, when faced with opposition, he often relented. (Apparently, Roosevelt was unwilling to risk a confrontation with the proponents of a worldwide internationalist strategy, whose support was vital in the struggle against the forces of isolationism.) Thus, although the president reacted favorably to the Japanese proposal for a summit meeting between Premier Fumimaro Konoye and himself when it was first suggested by Ambassador Nomura (on August 17, 1941), he was subsequently presuaded by Hull to change his mind. The evidence also indicates that during numerous cabinet meetings in which U.S. policy toward Japan was discussed, President Roosevelt played a neutral role, seeking a middle ground rather than acting as an initiator of policies or a clear-cut supporter of any of the others' views (Langer and Gleason, 1953: 697–708; Schroeder, 1958: 55–57; Pratt, 1964: 494–495).

Morgenthau's diary entry of July 19, 1940 (Book 284: July 18–21), provides a clear illustration of this behavioral pattern. The diary reveals that in the course of a "frantic" cabinet meeting, in which debate centered on the question of whether or not to place scrap metals and oil products on the list of "vital materials" not to be exported, Welles and Morgenthau (Hull was absent from the meeting because of an illness) "struck out at each other as soon as it began, and the President raised his hand in the air [and] refused to participate."

In view of this initial tendency to keep his distance from the competing factions and to seek compromises that would satisfy most of the partisan actors, President Roosevelt can be thought of as a typical "central decision maker" in the bureaucratic politics theory (Halperin, 1974: 24–25; Snyder and Diesing, 1977: 353; Thies, 1980: 355, 373). Generally exposed to "conflicting partisan pulls" (Snyder and Diesing, 1977: 352) and simultaneously preoccupied with a number of pressing foreign and domestic issues, this actor's activity was generally characterized by uncommitted thinking.

Not until the very eve of Pearl Harbor was this behavioral pattern somewhat modified. Faced with the continued pressures exerted by the partisan faction of Stimson, Morgenthau, and Hornbeck, the president (as well as Secretary of State Hull) ultimately acquiesced and supported their preferred course of action. Inevitably, it was this presidential decision that left the remaining members of the "blocking coalition" empty-handed in their all but doomed struggle to prevent at least some of the coercive measures advocated so relentlessly by the hard-line group.

In conclusion, the individuals involved in the formulation of American policy toward Japan did not comprise a homogeneous entity. Separated from one another in terms of their respective perceptions, resolve, and bargaining skill, various members of the Roosevelt entourage engaged in fierce competition for power and influence. On the eve of the Pacific War, this "bargaining game" finally produced a decisive victory for Stimson and Morgenthau (who were supported by the more militant Ickes), thus enabling the "majority coalition" to proceed apace toward the full implementation of its pre-existing images and convictions in the Pacific zone. In the final analysis, then, it was this convergence of conceptual vision and political and bureaucratic resources which eventually precipitated the transferral of certain images of the Pacific from the sphere of the abstract to the very real, tangible framework of the American-Japanese crisis as it unfolded in 1940 and 1941.

NOTES

1. The Roman Catholic clerics Bishop James E. Walsh and Father James M. Drought, who visited Japan in December 1940 on behalf of the Maryknoll Mission Society, were introduced to Japanese Foreign Minister Yosuke Matsuoka, Major General Akira Muto of the War Ministry, and other influential Japanese officials. Following these meetings, Walsh and Drought returned to Washington in January 1941 with a proposal for an American-Japanese agreement which "they [had] understood as coming directly from [the prime minister, Prince Fumimaro] Konoye and as representing his position." Their meeting with President Roosevelt and Secretary of State Cordell Hull, arranged through Postmaster-General Frank C. Walker, took place in the White House on January 23, 1941, and was followed by a series of unofficial contacts and meetings between Walsh and Drought and several members of the Japanese embassy in Washington. These meetings paved the way for the arrival in Washington (in February 1941) of Admiral Kichisaburo Nomura, who had been sent to negotiate an agreement with the United States (Butow, 1974).

THREE

Walsh, Drought, and Ickes: Two Conceptual Extremes

The individuals involved in the formulation of U.S. policy toward Japan differed widely in their views. Their thinking ranged from a naive, exaggerated optimism regarding the prospects of a lasting agreement with Japan, to a considerable pessimism and a deep-rooted suspicion of Japan, her leaders, and ultimate goals.

Bishop James E. Walsh, the Superior General of the Catholic Foreign Mission Society of America at Maryknoll, New York, and his second-in-command, Vicar General Father James M. Drought were examples of the soft-line, accommodative extreme of this conceptual spectrum. Walsh and Drought operated intermittently behind the diplomatic scene of American-Japanese relations, with Drought playing a consistently more active role than Walsh in his attempts to engender an American-Japanese settlement.

Walsh and Drought shared an idealistic vision of Japan, infused with empathy and understanding. Drought identified with the Japanese cause and Japan's foreign policy objectives, and consistently justified any action taken by the Japanese government up to the very eve of Pearl Harbor. As early as 1934 he expressed the view that "if treated with a spirit of dignified equality and an absence of suspicious fear [Japan] will be a good neighbor" (quoted in Butow, 1974: 53). Seven years later, incensed by an article in the *Herald Tribune* in which Walter Lippmann attacked former President Hoover and several other Republican leaders for being complacent in the face of the "desperately real problem" posed

17

by Japan in the Pacific, Drought relayed to Lippmann his conviction that there existed an American conspiracy to deliberately provoke Japan into a confrontation with the United States in the Pacific.

> There seems [Drought said] to be a conspiracy to entice Japan into actions which may be characterized as aggressive in order that advantage may be taken of public opinion to enter the war against Hitler through the back door of the Far East. I say that a conspiracy seems to exist because an accurate knowledge of Far Eastern conditions reveals no menace to the interests of the United States. On the contrary, our recent policy in the Far East has been aggressive. . . . It is a poor diplomacy that can find no solution but war; it is a wretched morality that forces a war with a disguised purpose. (quoted in Butow, 1974: 248)

Furthermore, Drought, predisposed as he was "to look at matters as the Japanese did" (Butow, 1974: 99), personally drafted numerous memoranda in which he approached the Far Eastern crisis from a distinctly Japanese perspective. Drought hoped that these "working analyses" would provide the impetus for an American-Japanese understanding. He was relentless in his effort (which proved abortive) to persuade the Roosevelt administration to accept his blueprint for peace in the Pacific as a basis for negotiations. Indeed, so committed was Drought to his vision of Japan as a friendly neighbor which posed no menace to American vital interests, that he went so far as to advise Japanese Foreign Minister Yosuke Matsuoka (in a memorandum submitted on December 5, 1940) "to make no present concessions [to the United States] on [the Japanese] military and political position in China [and the] Axis Alliance." Instead, Drought envisaged a political structure in eastern, central, and northern China which would "leave [the Japanese] position substantially unchanged but which could be presented [as] acceptable to American public opinion" (Butow, 1974: 82).

Similarly, Bishop Walsh consistently offered an extreme soft-line interpretation of Japan's behavior in the Pacific. Claiming in November 1940 that "I love the Japanese people as I love my own. . . . and I shall do all I can for their benefit" (quoted in Butow, 1974:), he argued that "the harsh talk [by the Japanese government] is for home consumption, lest the Government be supplanted by a group of Extremists. A bid for friendly settlement is being clearly made [in Tokyo]."

As to the sources of Drought and Walsh's profound feelings of sympathy and friendship toward Japan, it appears that personal experiences converged with organizational interests. Certainly Drought—as his message to Matsuoka of December 5, 1940 implies—was personally attracted to Japanese culture, to which he had been exposed since his first mission to the Far East in 1924. But Drought and Walsh were also clearly motivated in their search for an American-Japanese rapprochement by a cluster of narrow organizational considerations. Specifically, the two prominent leaders of the Maryknoll Society feared that a further deterioration in the Pacific might seriously jeopardize Maryknoll's missions and missionary activities in the Far East. Already in November 1940 the Japanese government had announced a change in policy toward Christian institutions within its jurisdiction, which required all of them to be headed by Japanese nationals. Similarly, Drought and Walsh were concerned lest the continued fighting in China cause further damage to Maryknoll missions there (Butow, 1974: 57, 62, 72). Thus they sought to dissociate Maryknoll from the increasingly coercive posture pursued by the Roosevelt administration toward Japan, while concurrently searching for ways to mitigate the intensely threatening crisis in American-Japanese relations.

As Drought pointed out in a letter to the Very Reverend John J. Burke, general secretary of the National Catholic Welfare Conference:

> The fact is that we are concerned with the continuity of our missions and the lives of our men. Accordingly, if a sharp antagonism is to be developed between the Japanese and Americans, we must feel bound to do all in our power to protect our own group even to the extent of making it clear to the Japanese authorities that we of Maryknoll do not share the political animosity which may actuate others. . . . I do not consider that we are any less American in that we are persistently Catholic. (quoted in Butow, 1974: 57)

Indeed, "aiding the Catholic cause as he saw it, and especially Maryknoll's share of it, was one of Drought's motivations [in entering the diplomatic scene], as was a desire to revamp American diplomacy" (Butow, 1974: 57).

This concern for "our missioners" was further reinforced by wider global-strategic considerations which revolved around the concept of an American-Japanese condominium in the Far East as a bulwark against "the twin evils of European imperialism and communism." Thus, in

Drought's thinking not only would an American-Japanese settlement guarantee the Society's interests and institutions in Japan and China; it would also place both countries "in so dominant a position as to minimize the importance of the European area for years to come." In Drought's words (taken from his memorandum to Matsuoka dated December 5, 1940), if such a settlement could be reached

> we would not only prevent the Far Eastern extension of the European conflict, but we would *immunize the Far East* against it. It is even possible that our two countries might become the final arbitrators of the outcome of the European War. Moreover, by such common action and agreement, we would create a friendly and intimate American relationship which would eliminate the likelihood of armed conflict with the United States and thereby strengthen our position against Russia which will remain, for years or generations, a doubtful quantity. (quoted in Butow, 1974: 84; italics in original)

An example of the hard-line conceptual spectrum was Secretary of the Interior Harold Ickes, who was, before the end of November 1941, the only member of the cabinet who advocated launching an attack upon Japan. Ickes was committed to a liberal philosophy; he was a leading member of the progressive wing of President Roosevelt's coalition and a staunch supporter of the New Deal. He was therefore predisposed to resent *any* manifestation of the forces of totalitarianism.

> The True America [he observed in 1935] will not tolerate a dictatorship either of the right or of the left. Fascism and Communism are equally abhorrent to us. Both are tyrannies. Both should be resisted with all our strength. . . . Show me a Communist and I will show you a man who, equally with a Fascist, has no respect for the rights of the individual; who would destroy for the sake of destroying. (quoted in Schlesinger, 1960: 195)

Indeed, as a believer in the ideas of democracy and political reform in domestic affairs, the secretary of the interior consistently demonstrated profound animosity toward any power, domestic or external, which represented the very antithesis of his liberal worldview (Ickes, 1953: Vols. 1, 10; Schlesinger, 1960: 359–360). He was particularly incensed and profoundly alarmed by Hitler's early diplomatic successes in Europe, and by the consolidation of the German-Italian Axis.

Ickes's dedication to liberal principles thus merged with wider global-strategic considerations. These derived from his growing conviction that the United States was faced with a mounting worldwide threat created by the Axis nations (and their Japanese ally) and aimed at the disruption of the global balance of power. This acutely threatening vision of Nazism and fascism increasingly dominated Ickes's thinking during the latter half of the thirties and thus overshadowed his animosity toward Soviet totalitarianism. The secretary's diary entry of January 29, 1939, elucidates this approach comprehensively:

> If Hitler breaks loose, as there is reason to believe now that he will do that shortly, and if he attains his objective, this country is going to suffer tremendously. As the President pointed out, Hitler will not have to control all of Europe and South America in order to make it difficult for us economically. For instance, the Argentine now exports eighty per cent of her products to Germany and other European countries. If Hitler can dominate the major part of Europe, he can serve notice on the Argentine that unless it accepts fascist principles and yields to fascistic economic domination, all of her exports to Europe will be cut off. No one need hesitate long to surmise what the answer would be in that event. And the same situation would exist with respect to other South American countries. They could be turned against us and we, in spite of our wealth and resources, would be powerless to do anything except to retire within our own territory, there to get along as best we could. (1953: Vol. 2, 568)

This conviction that the preservation of the global balance of power (and the protection of democratic structures) was of paramount importance to the United States, and that an eventual war between the forces of the status quo and those of revision and fascism was inevitable, led Ickes to oppose *any* factor that he perceived as disrupting the existing balance of power and encroaching upon democratic regimes and institutions. Thus, once he perceived Japan as being an integral part of this worldwide threat, he immediately labeled her an aggressive enemy. Starting in 1937 Ickes believed that the Japanese were irrevocably committed to the policies and ultimate goals of the Axis powers; therefore he advocated the launching of an attack upon Japan. Such an attack, he insisted, was a necessary preventive measure, which would also provide a convenient "back door" for entering the war against Germany.

Ickes comprehensively articulated his notions regarding the desirability of a preventive strike against Japan as early as December 28, 1937. Writing six days after the *Panay* incident (in which an American gunboat was sunk by the Japanese on the upper Yangtze River), he stated in his diary:

> Pacifist though I am, I am becoming imbued with the idea that sooner or later the democracies of the world, if they are to survive, will have to join issue—armed issue—with the fascist nations. This will mean that America and Japan will be at war, and if that ever is to happen, aren't we strategically in a better position now than we will be after Japan has strengthened her hand militarily and perhaps replenished her treasury with the spoils of China? If we should strike now, could not we put Japan in her place at a smaller cost in life and treasure than might be possible at any time thereafter? Whatever decision is made will necessarily be a grave and eventful one. (1953: Vol. 2, 276)

Nearly four years later, he similarly reflected:

> For a long time I have believed that our best entrance into the war would be by way of Japan. Undoubtedly we are nearer this eventuality than ever before. Japan has no friends in this country, but China has. And, of course, if we go to war against Japan, it will inevitably lead us to war against Germany. (1954: Vol. 3, 630)

The premise behind Ickes's continued advocacy of a preventive strike against Japan was most clearly and comprehensively articulated in his diary entry of November 21, 1941. So uninhibited was Ickes in elucidating the basis of his strategy that it is worthwhile to quote him at some length:

> The President remarked to me that he wished to know whether Japan was playing poker or not. He was not sure whether or not Japan had a gun up its sleeve. My reply was that I had no doubt that sooner or later, depending upon the progress of Germany, Japan would be at our throats; as for me, when I knew that I was going to be attacked, I preferred to choose my own time and occasion. I asked the President whether he had any doubt that Japan would attack Siberia if the Germans overcame

the Russians. He said that he hadn't.

I felt that by going to war with Japan now we would soon be in a position where a large part of our navy, as well as of the British Navy and of the Dutch East Indies Navy, could be released for service in the Atlantic. The President's feeling was that Japan would draw herself in and that she was too far away to be attacked. It seemed to me that the President had not yet reached the state of mind where he is willing to be aggressive as to Japan. (1954: Vol. 3, 649)

Other prominent cabinet members, such as Secretaries Stimson and Morgenthau, were convinced that Japan, when confronted by American firmness, would yield to the pressures exerted upon her and consequently adopt a much more conciliatory policy. Ickes, in contrast, hoped that the maintaining of a coercive posture by the United States would be a prelude to war. Ickes was not unique among American policy makers in viewing the Pacific theater as but one facet of a menacing, rapidly developing global crisis. However, on the *tactical* level of choosing the means necessary to cope with this threat, he clearly differed from all other administration officials engaged in the decision-making process. While many decision makers believed that war with Germany was inevitable, only Ickes insisted that war against Japan was the preferable course of action in order to restore the global balance of power.

This unique approach was clearly and repeatedly manifested during the period immediately preceding Pearl Harbor. Thus on the eve of the Pacific War, Ickes continuously argued (1954: Vol. 3, 649) that Japan was using diplomatic negotiations with the United States only as a mask behind which she patiently awaited the opportunity to carry out her sinister design—to "be at our throats" and "sink us without trace." Convinced that any negotiations with Japan were in vain, he strongly believed that drastic economic sanctions should be imposed upon her as a prelude to war and as a means of reducing her prospects of success in the approaching conflict. As the secretary of the interior wrote to the president on June 23, 1941:

To embargo oil to Japan would be as popular a move in all parts of the country as you could make. Recent expressions of sentiment have demonstrated how the people feel on this subject. *There might develop from the embargoing of oil to Japan such a situation as would make it not only possible but easy, to get into this war in an effective way.* And if we should thus indirectly be brought in, we would avoid the criticism that we had gone in as an ally of communistic Russia. (PSF, 1941: Box 75, Harold L. Ickes; italics added)

In persistently advocating a posture of harsh economic sanctions, Ickes frequently clashed with the State Department, criticizing its "hesitant and cautious approach" (1954: Vol. 3, 298, 338, 473, 537). As he wrote to Roosevelt on June 23, 1941 (PSF, Box 75, Harold L. Ickes): "I have followed the diplomatic game with intense interest from the time that Italy invaded Abyssinia, and I think that our State Department has made mistake after mistake. I believe that it has done so particularly with respect to Japan, and I don't think that this continuing mistake will get us anywhere except into trouble."

Indeed, although—as we shall later see—Secretary of State Hull was no less devoted than Secretary Ickes to such principles as peaceful change and nonaggression, the two cabinet members differed sharply on the appropriate tactics for meeting the worldwide revisionist challenge to Western democracy and to American national security. Whereas Hull initially pursued a cautious policy in the Pacific, Ickes—whose overall approach to politics was much more assertive—repeatedly insisted that the United States "choose its own time and occasion [to attack]." Although Hull became increasingly pessimistic during the summer of 1941 about the prospects of an American-Japanese settlement, his growing disillusionment with Japan's behavior did not lead him even then to advocate a preventive strike. (It led him, however, to abandon his restrained approach, and to give support to the *deterrent* posture advocated by Secretaries Stimson and Morgenthau.)

A juxtaposition of Ickes's perceptions of the international system and the worldviews adhered to by Walsh and Drought indicates that while the secretary of the interior was acutely sensitive to the threat posed by the Axis powers (and their Japanese ally) to the global balance of power (and to the principles of liberal democracy), the two clergymen were primarily concerned with an altogether different form of European menace to American interests which stemmed from Western imperialism and from Soviet communism. "It is my feeling," observed Drought to the Bishop of Reno, Nevada (quoted in Butow, 1974: 57–58), "that, as American citizens, we should not permit ourselves to be misled by the subtle diplomacy of the British and French and Russians into acting as the police agent for the protection of their own interests in the Far East."

However, for all this incompatibility in terms of specific content, the two extremes shared a similar *structure* of belief systems. This led Drought, Walsh, as well as Ickes to strongly adhere to their preconceived, fixed images. Indeed, in evaluating these two extremes of optimism and skepticism regarding Japanese-American relations, it is evident that Drought, Walsh, and Ickes had in common a "closed" belief system, in the sense that they all tended to assimilate new information concerning Japan in a manner corresponding with their established views. In the case of Walsh and Drought, their relentless drive to engender a rapprochement between the United States and Japan led them to overlook fundamental sources of disagreement between the two countries. Their naive wish that the world would conform to their harmonious image led them to obfuscate latent (and occasionally even manifest) controversies in American-Japanese relations. As a result of their overoptimistic reports to Washington, in which they reiterated their belief in Japan's readiness to make significant concessions on several central issues, a number of high-ranking American officials termporarily adopted some unfounded ideas as to the extent of Japan's eagerness for compromise.

Similarly, during their visit to Japan, Walsh and Drought encouraged several high-ranking Japanese officials to form more optimistic views concerning the attitude of the United States than were justified by fact. Drought, for example, appears to have mentioned more than once that he was acting with the approval of "top personnel" in the American government. As a result, Japanese officials regarded his statements as representing President Roosevelt's personal views.

Eventually, this unfounded optimism and the proclivity to obfuscate sources of disagreement which strained American-Japanese relations resulted in a credibility gap between the two governments and aggravated an already confused and tense situation. Thus, while Walsh and Drought paved the way for Ambassador Nomura's mission to the United States, they also created serious misunderstandings and a communication gap.[1] In Butow's words,

> Professional diplomats may not have all the answers, but they generally have more and better answers than amateurs are likely to provide. . . . War in the Pacific was not inevitable in 1941, but the backdoor diplomacy of [Drought, Walsh, and their associates] made an amicable settlement of the Far Eastern crisis harder to obtain. [They] were a distracting and disruptive element. Their will o' the wisp activities ate into the time and energy of men with professional training and experience who might otherwise

have been free to develop, on their own, workable formulas of compromise. . . .

In playing the private brokers for peace, [they] enormously complicated the Hull-Nomura conversations, making them more muddled and ineffectual than they would otherwise have been. In the end, the old and battered and foundering ship of Japanese-American relations went plummeting to the bottom of the sea—not simply a victim of dastardly destruction from without, as the President saw it, but also of unintentional scuttling from within—a tragedy that might more easily have been averted if only [Drought, Walsh, and associates] had never been permitted to set foot on board that already badly listing vessel at such a critical moment in world history. (1974: 317, 319–320)

At the other extreme, Ickes's propensity to think in categories of black and white and to cling persistently to his fixed image of Japan as an inherently aggressive homogeneous entity led him to overlook the highly complex nature of both American-Japanese relations and the Japanese decision-making process. Ickes's image of Japan was so "closed" that he was predisposed to distort information so as to minimize the clash between incoming stimuli and previous expectations. Consequently, certain pieces of information that deviated from Ickes's pre-existing image (to which, like Walsh and Drought, he irrevocably adhered) were either systematically excluded or distorted. In his deep mistrust of the Japanese leaders, Ickes tended to read wicked intentions into certain Japanese diplomatic moves when in fact no such intentions existed. He therefore tended to compress the highly complex and differentiated events that unfolded on the American-Japanese scene into one preconceived pattern (see, in this connection, Jervis, 1968: 475; Falkowski, 1979: 54–55; Thies, 1980: 363).

For example, although unacquainted with all the relevant information, Ickes (1954: Vol. 3, 629) did not hesitate to interpret the fall of Konoye's second cabinet and the establishment, on October 16, 1941, of a new cabinet headed by General Hideki Tojo as prime minister as an undisputed indication that "Japan [was] again rattling her sword in her sheath." This view sharply contradicted the assessment of the naval attaché in Tokyo, Lieutenant Colonel Harry I. T. Creswell, who, in his intelligence report of October 20, 1941, observed that the establishment of Tojo's cabinet is not regarded as necessarily indicating any radical changes in Japanese policy, at least as far as the immediate future is concerned. . . . Although a good deal of foreign opinion is inclined to view the accession to the premiership of an Army officer on the active list with some concern, it is not felt that such anxiety is necessarily justified. General Tojo is a known conservative [and] is considered as having a breadth of vision which would appear to preclude any action of the more radical or extreme type. (in Hopkins, 1935–45: Military Intelligence Reports, Far Eastern Documents: Box 193)

And indeed, the new cabinet continued, at least temporarily, to demonstrate the same conciliatory spirit toward the United States that had characterized Konoye's second cabinet.

Thus it was Tojo's cabinet which, in early November, formulated and submitted new proposals to the United States, some of which represented "the farthest point [to which Japan] had gone in offering concessions," in a desperate, last-ditch effort to reach an agreement and avoid war. As Schroeder points out,

There can be little doubt that not only Nomura and Kurusu [a special envoy to the United States, who served there temporarily as Nomura's assistant] in Washington, but also Togo [foreign minister in Tojo's cabinet] and Tojo were earnestly trying to gain acceptance of the Japanese proposition and thus striving, within limits, to reach an agreement with the U.S. and avert war. (1958: 76)

Hsu, who studied the last phase of the American-Japanese negotiations, concurred, maintaining (1952: 302) that Tojo was chosen premier primarily because of the emperor's desire to find someone who could effectively control the army and thus be in a position to reach a viable agreement with the United States: "in contrast to the allegation of many people that Tojo was warlike, he was committed to a policy of peace at the beginning, an attitude which at once disappointed the Germans, who had expected him to be a military interventionist who would check the American convoying operations in European waters."

Yet Ickes's attitude of suspicion toward Japanese intentions led him to conclude that "it was clear as crystal that these [American-Japanese] conversations had been merely a ruse to hold our attention while Japan was preparing its attack. Undoubtedly, these two Japanese diplomats must have known that they were being used as decoys" (1954: Vol. 3, 663).

None of these assumptions was supported by factual evidence. On the contrary, both Nomura and Kurusu were motivated by a strong desire to prevent war and were sincere in their efforts to reach an agreement. Far from being involved in a conspiracy to prolong negotiations in order to camouflage Japan's aggressive intentions, they exceeded their government's instructions in their eagerness to reach an understanding with the United States (Hull, 1948, Vol. 2, 987; Hsu, 1952: 304).

Ickes's staunch adherence to his one-dimensional image of Japan and his predisposition to interpret any step taken by the Japanese government in a way that preserved this image, prevented him from recognizing the divergent points of view which existed within almost every Japanese cabinet. Since he failed to differentiate among the various influential social and political groups in Japan which advocated different policy lines toward the United States, he continued to the very end to adhere to his "background images" of unity and coordination, and these always dominated his information processing and his derivative policy preferences (see in this connection Bronfenbrenner, 1961: 45–56; White, 1965: 241; Jervis, 1976; Snyder and Diesing, 1977: 329–337; Thies, 1980: 347, 363; Lockhart, 1981).

Ickes's advocacy of a preventive war against Japan was not shared by other cabinet members. Nevertheless, one finds a considerable congruence between his general approach to international politics and the views held by Secretaries Stimson and Morgenthau, as well as those held by State Department political advisor Stanley Hornbeck. Although not as extremely one-dimensional in its thinking as Ickes, this group shared most of his views and policy recommendations. It is these views which we shall examine in the following chapter.

NOTES

1. Ambassador Nomura (who was not an experienced diplomat at the time of his mission to the United States) committed the same error of ignoring those facts which did not conform with his personal desires. Although his views were not as simplistic as those of Walsh and Drought, Nomura nevertheless adopted a conciliatory and optimistic view of the prospects of reaching an agreement with the United States and emphasized in his reports those American gestures which indicated friendliness and readiness to compromise—even though these were sometimes taken out of context and were frequently exaggerated. At the same time, he *did not* report to his

government the content of some meetings (and even the content of one American proposal) in which the Americans demonstrated firmness. In his eagerness to read into America's policy statements what he wanted to find, Nomura "desperately sought in [Hull's remarks] some indication of a conciliatory spirit," despite the fact that "the Secretary's tone was always uncompromising if not belligerent" (Iriye, 1967: 219). Furthermore, on a number of occasions (such as on September 4, 1941) the ambassador—without any instructions from Tokyo—took it upon himself to make several changes in wording before delivering Japanese proposals and messages, and in other instances he presented to Hull his own personal proposals, which reflected his preconceived notions rather than the official attitudes of the Japanese government (Hosoya, 1973: 158). Indeed, as soon as Nomura's independent role as a negotiator—which inevitably created a serious communication gap between Washington and Tokyo—became known to Japan's Foreign Ministry, he was instructed by Foreign Minister Toyoda on September 25, 1941, "to refrain from adding to or deleting from any message on your own without consulting us first" (Hosoya, 1973: 159).

FOUR

Stimson, Morgenthau, and Hornbeck: The Global Approach

THE PARAMETERS

The image of Japan held in the late thirties and early forties by Secretaries Stimson and Morgenthau as well as by Stanley Hornbeck reflected certain personal and organizational experiences, all of which merged into a coherent, shared worldview. This revolved around the notion that "the problem of peace and national relations in the Far East is today directly connected with the same problems in Europe" (Stimson's letter to President Roosevelt, November 15, 1937, in President's Personal File [PPF], Box 20: Henry L. Stimson). The group was convinced that the Axis powers and their allies were pursuing a worldwide policy of disrupting the global balance of power. Stimson, Morgenthau, and Hornbeck believed that this coordinated European-Asian axis was manifested in various political and military moves initiated by Japan, such as the conquest of Hankow and Canton, which were aimed at establishing Japanese control over the rich resources of the Dutch East Indies. In their minds, these actions coincided with such developments in Europe as the Munich Conference of September 1938 and the German victories of the following two years. They maintained that the United States was called upon to react, principally through military cooperation with England.

Toward the end of the thirties, it became even clearer to Stimson, Morgenthau, and Hornbeck that the East Asian situation was not an isolated phenomenon but part of a menacing world crisis. Their assumption that a link existed between the concurrent developments in Europe and Asia became more pronounced following the conclusion, in September 1940, of the Tripartite Pact between Germany, Italy, and Japan. As Iriye observes:

> There emerged the possibility, as they saw it, that the aggressive nations, in particular Germany and Japan, might band together and collectively menace the status quo and peace in the whole world. . . . Aggression in Asia [was, therefore, to] be resisted to discourage lawless action in Europe. (1967: 203)

On the eve of the Pacific War, this global perspective led Stimson, Morgenthau, and Hornbeck to object to any country which in their view allied itself with the Axis's effort to disrupt the balance of power. Once Japan was so perceived, their posture toward her changed accordingly.

A distinction can be drawn between Stimson and Morgenthau on the one hand and Hornbeck on the other. The former largely supported a major emphasis on Europe; the latter was one of the strongest of the "Asia-firsters" in the sense that he perceived the Pacific zone as the area in which the revisionist powers could most successfully be deterred. Thus, while all three globalist-realists pictured Japan as closely associated with Germany and Italy in the worldwide threat to the balance of power, Hornbeck wanted the United States to concentrate its main political and military efforts in the Pacific. Beyond this distinction, however, Stimson, Morgenthau, and Hornbeck were all motivated by a global approach which led them to perceive the Pacific as merely one manifestation of the global conflict between the "three aggressor nations" and the status quo powers.[1]

It is clear that in the thinking of these influential members of President Roosevelt's policy elite, this perception of extreme threat was translated into a strategy of economic and political coercion designed to compel Japan to abandon the major premises of its foreign policy (i.e., continued advance to the south, continued occupation of China, and rapprochement with the Axis powers). More specifically, during most of this period Stimson, Morgenthau, and Hornbeck recommended a posture which was closely patterned on the "try and see" variant of coercive diplomacy (George, Hall, and Simons, 1971: 26). In this version, pressure is exerted *incrementally* by a series of limited punitive measures intended to convince the challenger that the coercing party has both the will and the power "to inflict considerable damage upon something which the challenger values more than the subject of the dispute" (Lauren, 1979: 193). Indeed, these members of the Roosevelt entourage remained fully committed up to the very eve of Pearl Harbor to the premises of the "try and see" approach. They believed that the imposition on Japan of increasingly more comprehensive economic sanctions was bound to ultimately contain Japan by eroding its motivation to persist in its expansionist behavior.

We now turn to the detailed analysis of these premises.

HENRY MORGENTHAU, JR.

The global vision of the threat confronting the United States was comprehensively outlined by Morgenthau shortly after the conclusion of the Munich Conference. (Morgenthau's *Presidential Diaries*, 1938–1939: Book 1, January 1, 1938–July 31, 1939). In a memorandum submitted to the President of October 17, 1938, Morgenthau portrayed the Pacific as but one facet of an integrated worldwide revisionist scheme seeking to encroach upon democracy:

> Japan at first wanted only Manchuria, then Northern China; now she will not be content with less than the whole of China. Italy wanted only Ethiopia; now she wants control of North Africa, Germany wanted only equality in armament, then the remilitarization of the Rhineland, then Austria, then Czechoslovakia, now colonies. [In this light] we should learn the lesson which the history of the last years has to teach us. Let us not repeat the short-sighted mistakes of Britain and France. . . . Let us, while we can peacefully do so, try to check the aggressors. . . . Let us not be in the position of having to compound with them. Let it not be necessary for the President of the U.S. to fly to Tokyo in a humble manner and plead with the Mikado that he be content with half the Philippines rather than wage war for the whole. Such a possibility may seem ridiculous now, but no more ridiculous than Chamberlain's flight to Berlin would have seemed seven years ago.

Morgenthau feared that Japan's demands on China, unabating after her conquest of Manchuria in 1931, might "threaten the peace of the Orient and of the World." Thus, in a classic balance-of-power pose, he advocated a policy of monetary aid to China in order "to cultivate the Chinese will to resist Japan." Otherwise, he observed in 1934, the United States "would lose all influence in the Orient, leaving the area entirely to Japan and Great Britain" (quoted in Blum, 1970: 99). Perceiving the Japanese challenge to China as inextricably related to "the worldwide threat to liberal democracy" (Gardner, 1973: 264), Morgenthau was therefore predisposed to support any power—including China (and later Britain)—which sought to resist fascist aggression or global schemes which aimed at encroaching upon the free world (Tuchman, 1970: 189; Gardner, 1973: 285). Against this backdrop of preoccupation with the limits and components of the balance of power, it is hardly surprising that Morgenthau's views on Japan were seen as "rash and rigid" by "several State Department officers" (Gardner, 1973: 264).

In addition to his pre-existing worldview, which set the parameters of his approach to the Far East, Morgenthau's specific attitudes toward Japan and China were futher affected by his departmental perspective and organizational background. Stimson and Hornbeck's approach was (as we shall soon see) profoundly influenced by the firsthand experience in such emotion-laden episodes as the Manchurian crisis. Morgenthau's thinking, on the other hand, at least partially reflected certain narrow organizational predilections. Motivated by such parochial considerations, Morgenthau (who in 1933 headed the Farm Credit Administration) strongly supported a $50 million credit to China for wheat and cotton purchases. He was unimpressed with the objections raised by the State Department's Far Eastern Division (which argued that the credit would "further anger the Japanese") and insisted that "even if the loan were never repaid, it might boost the value of American agriculture stocks as much as $100 million, forestalling Agriculture Secretary Henry Wallace's proposal to plow under standing crops to create scarcity pressures upon the law of supply and demand" (Gardner, 1973: 268).

Similarly, the secretary of the treasury recommended a policy of massive economic assistance to China, convinced as he was that American aid to China would, in addition to being "an instrument of political support" (quoted in Blum, 1970: 99), be beneficial "to American economic well-being" (Gardner, 1973: 270). During the period preceding the Sino-Japanese war, this policy culminated in the concurrent approval in 1936 of the "silver purchase program" and of a new Export-Import Bank credit of $50 million to China (Gardner, 1973: 274).

While sectorial considerations may have played a significant role in shaping Morgenthau's initial approach to the Far East, they later merged with, and were by and large overshadowed by, wider balance-of-power considerations. Morgenthau was profoundly alarmed by such developments as the Japanese invasion of China and the *Panay* incident; and perceived the escalating Far Eastern crisis as an integral part of the worldwide "totalitarian challenge to liberal democracy" (Gardner, 1973: 264) and hence to the national security of the United States. Thus he adopted an increasingly belligerent attitude toward Japan.

As early as December 1937, being incensed by the sinking of the *Panay* gunboat by the Japanese, Morgenthau initiated a series of extensive interdepartmental staff meetings which explored the legal and practical ways to impose far-reaching sanctions upon Japan. Convinced that "we've got to begin to inch in on those [Japanese] boys" (*The Morgenthau Diary*, 1937: Book 103, December 17–21), the secretary of the treasury predicted—in his staff meeting of December 17, 1937—that unless the United States took vigorous and determined action it would have to confront the Japanese challenge

> in the Philippines, then in Hawaii, and then in Panama. [As he further told his senior advisors on December 17, 1937]: I think it's a time to call a halt when a United States battleship [*Panay*] has been sunk and three of our people have been killed. For us to let them put their sword into our insides and sit there and take it and like it, and not do anything about it, I think is un-American. . . . I feel very, very strongly that this is the time for the United States Government to tell Japan, "Now you've got to behave yourselves, and if you don't, we'll take the necessary steps to make you behave yourselves." Because if we don't do that it's only a matter of five or ten years before we'll have them on our neck. (*The Morgenthau Diary*, 1937: Book 103, December 17–21)

Morgenthau, then, believed that a firm, retaliatory course in the Pacific was bound to deter Tokyo. By invoking the exchange restrictions under the 1933 ammendment to the Trading-with-the-Enemy Act he moved rapidly, in the wake of the *Panay* incident, to establish the necessary administrative machinery and infrastructure for effectually prohibiting banking and foreign exchange transactions and monetary exports in which the Japanese Government was directly or indirectly involved (see staff meetings of December 17, 18, 21, 1937, on "possible control of Japan's credits and purchasing channels in the U.S." in *The Morgenthau*

Diary, 1937: Book 103, December 17–21).

In the short run and within the delimited context of the *Panay* crisis, the elaborate plans for controlling Japan's credits in the United States, which were prepared by Morgenthau and his assistants (and primarily by Herman Oliphant), were in fact not translated into action. President Roosevelt, satisfied with Japan's apology and willingness to pay indemnities for damages and loss of life, decided to reject Morgenthau's recommendation of economic sanctions against Japan.

However, less than four years after the *Panay* episode had receded into the background of American-Japanese relations, the secretary of the treasury ultimately succeeded in implementing at least some of the ideas which emerged from the intradepartmental discussions held in December 1937. As the crisis in the Pacific escalated sharply in July 1941, Morgenthau took full advantage of such pre-existing organizational "action plans" as the scheme for imposing a de facto embargo on exports to Japan by "refusing to issue licenses" (Oliphant's words, taken from a staff meeting dated December 17, 1937. *The Morgenthau Diary*, 1937: Book 103, December 17–21). With the support of the powerful secretary of war, Henry Stimson, Morgenthau implemented economic sanctions that required that "all transactions in yen or transfers of payments involving the Japanese Government, as well as transfers involving private individuals" be licensed by the Treasury Department. That this "license system" amounted in fact to an embargo (as no such licenses were ever issued by the department) was, of course, an integral part of Morgenthau's original design.

HENRY L. STIMSON

It is evident that in addition to Secretary of War Stimson's global perspective, which a priori dictated animosity and opposition toward *any* power participating in the conspiracy to disrupt the balance of power, his *specific* attitudes toward Japan in 1940 and 1941 (both on the effective and evaluative levels) were affected by his personal involvement in the Manchurian crisis of 1931–1932, when he was serving as secretary of state in President Herbert Hoover's cabinet. In later years, the lessons which Stimson drew from his perceptions of Japan's behavior during that crisis profoundly influenced his attitude toward American-Japanese relations and were fully incorporated into his sharply delineated vision of the worldwide revisionist attempt to dominate both the Atlantic and the Pacific.

Not only did this episode affect Stimson's thinking in establishing certain fixed images (to which he would adhere in future years), but it also became the source of sweeping analogies which he later applied to the American-Japanese crisis of 1940–1941. Indeed, by virtue of its magnitude and perceived implications, the Manchurian crisis can be thought of as the "trigger event" (Jervis, 1968: 469–472, 1976: 220, 237, 271, 275, 308; Touval 1973: 17) which acutely sensitized Stimson to the dangers inherent in pursuing an accommodative policy toward Japan; and thus prompted him, later, "to see ambiguous stimuli as indicating another instance of this kind of event" (Jervis, 1968: 471). As Jervis further observes (in the context of his analysis of the sources of misperception):

> Concepts will be supplied by the actor's previous experiences. . . . A state's previous unfortunate experience with a type of danger can sensitize it to other examples of that danger. While this sensitivity may lead the state to avoid the mistake it committed in the past, it may also lead it mistakenly to believe that the present situation is like the past one. (1968: 470)

Thus a brief analysis of the Manchurian crisis and Stimson's reaction to it is in order. During the first few weeks following the Mukden incident of September 18, 1931, Stimson's attitude toward Japan was cautious, as he was capable of recognizing the valid grievances held by both sides to the dispute. This preliminary accommodative strategy was consistent with the moderate (and occasionally even friendly) policy line which he had sought to implement in the Pacific since his appointment as secretary of state in 1929. Stimson most clearly articulated this position at the close of the London Naval Conference of 1930 when he spoke of "our good neighbors across the Pacific, and of the continuous growth of our friendship with that great nation [Japan] toward which we have grown to look for stability and progress in the Far East" (quoted in Rappaport, 1963: 34–35). According to Stimson's account of the early phase of the crisis, his initial course of action was to search for a formula which would "save Japan's face" and give the Japanese government "time to settle [the dispute] by themselves with China" (Stimson's *Diary*, 1931: Vol. 18, September 9–October 30, entry of September 23).

Stimson was sensitive to the dangers inherent in adopting an irreconcilable posture toward Japan, and thus opposed the imposition of any settlement upon Japan by the League of Nations or by any other outside force. Instead he urged direct Sino-Japanese negotiations. He feared that any other policy would "cause a flare-up in Japan" and arouse nationalistic feelings that could only strengthen the Japanese military and further weaken the civil authorities. Convinced that the crisis was initiated by "a group of military subordinates [who launched] a widely extended movement of aggression in defiance of orders from the Japanese government" (quoted in Rappaport, 1963: 26), the secretary of state was thus initially capable of distinguishing among the various factions operating on the Japanese political and military scene. As he wrote in his diary (1931: Vol. 18, September 9–October 30) on September 28, 1931: "The Japanese are very much pleased with the consideration I have shown them in preventing too rough a treatment while Shidehara [Japan's prime minister] and Wakatsuki [Japan's foreign minister] are trying to get their army rebels under control."

But Stimson's initial caution and sensitivity to the domestic situation in Japan did not last long. His conciliatory attitude evaporated during the following months as his perception of the escalating Manchurian crisis gradually changed. Whereas during the first two weeks following the Mukden incident Stimson repeatedly emphasized that his government was not attempting "to go into the question of right and wrong, [was] not taking sides, [and was] playing no favorites" (quoted in Current, 1950: 75), this moderation progressively eroded during October and November. Upon hearing that Japanese aircraft were bombing the city of Chinchow in southern Manchuria, Stimson for the first time referred to Japan as an "aggressive power which ought to be contained by the U.S." (Stimson and Bundy, 1948: 227–228; Current, 1950: 76; Morison, 1960: 313). The shift in the content of Stimson's cognitive map of the Pacific zone appeared for the first time in his diary entry of October 8, 1931:

> I am afraid we have got to take a firm ground and aggressive stand toward Japan. . . . The President [Hoover] has been so immersed in his domestic crisis and the tremendous work he has been doing there, that he hasn't envisaged this situation at all; and I don't think he realizes what it means to him in his administration to have Japan run amok and play havoc with its peace treaties. (1931: Vol. 18, September 9–October 30)

Indeed, an examination of Stimson's other diary entries of October 1931 reveals his ever-growing doubts as to whether his initial conciliatory posture would be sufficient to terminate the crisis. This in turn reflected deeper doubts as to the accuracy of his original perception of Japan as "a peaceful and friendly neighbor."

Stimson's outlook was manifested with considerably greater confidence during November, when the Manchurian crisis further escalated into an event of great magnitude. Thus, incensed by the Japanese attack on Tsitsihor and the renewed onslaught on Chinchow (which convinced him that his initial belief that "the Japanese Army [was] running amok and defying its own Government" [quoted in Current, 1950: 75] was wrong), Stimson now expressed a growing willingness to completely abandon his original vision of the Japanese modus operandi and to pursue instead a posture which was predicated upon an indiscriminate perception of Japan as an inherently aggressive entity. On November 23, 1931, the latent finally became fully manifest as Stimson for the first time expressed *unqualified* support for an intransigent strategy as a means of restraining Japanese actions in Manchuria. He was becoming increasingly frustrated with the apparent failure of his initially accommodative strategy, and was convinced that "the United States could not afford to abandon Chinese sovereignty and independence to Japanese aggression and exploitation" (Osgood, 1953: 353). He therefore embarked on a more assertive course which fully coincided with his newly formed vision of Japan. Indeed, Stimson's statements and actions from late November 1931 until his departure from office more than a year later indicate that there were no second thoughts and no deviations from his new policy line. Instead, he further consolidated his revised image of Japan, which was now juxtaposed with his romantic image of China (see in this connection Stimson's letter to President Roosevelt dated November 15, 1937, in PPF, Box 20: Henry L. Stimson).

One can note a basic similarity, if not a total congruency, between Stimson of 1931 and 1932, articulating his belief in the effectiveness of coercive diplomacy, and Stimson of a decade later. For example, on November 27, 1931, in a conversation with President Hoover, Stimson (*Diary*, 1931: Vol. 19, November 1–December 29) "pointed out . . . certain elements which existed in favor of an embargo [against Japan]." He further argued that "an embargo, if joined in by all the world against Japan, would be a very brief event. She would have to surrender very quickly." (However, President Hoover's opposition to the unilateral imposition of such an embargo forced the secretary of state to work strictly within the framework of the largely ineffective "nonrecognition" doctrine.) Writing in his diary on January 26, 1932, Stimson sharply criticized President Hoover's opposition to his deterrent policy (see also Osgood, 1953: 359; Divine, 1962: 26–30):

> I thought we had a right to rely upon the unconscious elements
> of our great size and military strength: that I knew Japan was
> afraid of that. . . . When you have a case where the chances are a
> thousand to one that you will not be drawn into a fight, I am
> willing to let our size and strength speak for itself and not to
> declaim publicly our willingness to fight if it becomes essential.
> (1932: Vol. 20, January 1–February 21)

Eight years later, this belief in coercive diplomacy remained unchanged. As Stimson (*Correspondence*, 1940) observed in his letter of April
4, 1940, to Chauncey J. Hamlin (of the Buffalo Museum of Science): "I do
not think. . . . that the Japanese would attack the Philippines even if we
put an embargo on raw materials for arms. All the evidence which I
have indicates that they are more afraid of war with us than anything
else." Being convinced that the failure of American diplomacy during
the Manchurian crisis had been caused largely by Hoover's reluctance to
use economic sanctions as a deterrent (Divine, 1962: 30), Stimson was
quick to draw conclusions from that episode about the weaknesses inherent in an accommodative posture in the Pacific and the necessity of
avoiding any subsequent indication of moderation: "It seemed to me," he
recalled later (*Diary*, 1939: 157), "that in future years I should not like to
face a verdict of history to the effect that a government to which I
belonged had failed to express itself adequately upon such a situation"
(see also Morison, 1960: 523).

In Jervis's terminology (1976: 274), Stimson's image of Japan became
overgeneralized as expectations established from behavior in one set of
circumstances (the Manchurian crisis) were carried over into quite different situations (the American-Japanese crisis of 1940–1941). In other
words, by seeking to avoid the policy which had failed to contain Japan
in Manchuria (namely, the posture of nonrecognition and moral embargo), Stimson staunchly supported—almost a decade later—a coercive
posture which was the antithesis of the restrained policy adhered to by
President Hoover in 1931 and 1932.

It is hardly surprising that the factor determining Stimson's behavior
toward Japan in 1940 and 1941 was his strong belief that the imposition
of drastic economic sanctions upon Japan—combined with such military measures as the establishment in the Philippines of a base for the
newly developed four-engine bomber—would constitute the most effective deterrent measure available to the United States (see, e.g., Stimson's
letter to President Roosevelt dated October 21, 1941, in President's Secretary's File [PSF]: 1940–1941, Box 106, War Department). He was con-

vinced that once Japan was impressed by America's firm determination and deprived of some of her most vital necessities, she would succumb to the economic pressure and would consequently adopt a more conciliatory policy toward the United States (Langer and Gleason, 1953: 34–35; Hooker, 1965: 331; Hosoya, 1968: 97–112; Blum, 1970: 381–421; George, Hall, and Simons, 1971: 245; Russett, 1972: 92; Graebner, 1973: 45; Jervis, 1979: 296–307; Lauren 1979: 192; Betts, 1982: 42–50).

This belief in the effectiveness of coercive diplomacy was comprehensively articulated by Stimson in a letter published in the *New York Times* on January 11, 1940 (a copy of the letter is included in PPF, 1940: Box 20):

> The real responsibility [for the reluctance of the United States to impose comprehensive economic sanctions upon Japan] therefore rests . . . upon those political leaders who have tried to frighten our government from doing anything to prevent the wrong by warning them to do so would surely lead them into war with Japan.
>
> Experienced observers have promptly recognized and publicly stated that such a fear was without credible foundation; that the very last thing which the Japanese Government desires is a war with the U.S.; and that, on the contrary, every act and word of our government in respect of the Orient is followed with most anxious solicitude in Japan. . . . But the clearest demonstration [of Japan's restraint in the light of American firmness] came when our government, after a long period of forbearance with repeated violations of our own rights in China, took sudden and vigorous actions, and on July 26 last denounced the Japanese-American commercial treaty of 1911, to become effective six months from that date. . . . Did Japan bluster and threaten war after these abrupt and very direct warnings from our government? She did not. She at once put the brakes on the long series of aggressive acts of her agents against Americans in China; she promised to reopen the lower Yangtze River; she uttered other conciliatory statements. . . . Consequently [it is essential] to impress Japan with the seriousness of the feeling of our people [and to pass legislation that] would carry with it a weight of influence which would be far more effective in impressing the people of Japan with the sincerity of our purpose.

The premise behind this view was that Japan was most anxious to avoid war and that when confronted with a "bold and positive American policy" aimed at depriving her of vital raw materials she would act responsibly. "Whatever the risks of economic sanctions when used by other nations to serve other contingencies," observed Stimson in a letter to Senator Kay Pittman on April 25, 1939 (Stimson, *Correspondence*, 1939), "I entirely fail to see the dangers of their use by a nation as powerful as ours against another nation as susceptible to them as Japan is in her present condition."

Similarly, in a "Historical Memorandum as to Japan's relations with the United States which may have a bearing upon the present situation," which Stimson composed and on October 2, 1940, sent to his coalition partner, Morgenthau (*The Morgenthau Diary*, 1940: Book 318, October 2–3), the newly-appointed secretary of war asserted:

> Japan has historically shown that she can misinterpret a pacifistic policy of the United States for weakness. She has also historically shown that when the United States indicates by clear language and bold actions that she intends to carry out a clear and affirmative policy in the Far East, Japan will yield to that policy even though it conflicts with her own Asiatic policy and conceived interests. For the United States now to indicate either by soft words or inconsistent actions that she has no such clear and definite policy toward the Far East will only encourage Japan to bolder action.

STANLEY HORNBECK

Whereas Stimson's behavior in the course of the Pacific crisis of 1940–1941 was profoundly influenced by his involvement in the Manchurian crisis, Hornbeck's approach during the period preceding the Pacific War was apparently affected by his "Chinese experience." In 1909 Hornbeck accepted a teaching position at Chekiang Provincial College in Hangchow, where he stayed four years; and in 1913 he moved to Manchuria for a further year of teaching at Fengtien Law College in Mukden (Thomson, 1973: 82). His personal experience and continued exposure to Chinese culture later enabled Hornbeck to readily empathize with the Chinese viewpoint. As he asked rhetorically in 1927:

> To prevent the establishment of inequalities, to insure against
> the partition of China, to save China herself from internal dis-
> turbances and to guard against some new form of anti-foreign
> agitation which may affect all foreign nations alike injuriously,
> should not every nation which is in a position to do so exert it-
> self to restrain any other whose policies appear likely to insure
> some or all of these undesirable consequences? (quoted in Thom-
> son, 1973: 91)

These factors as well as the influence of Paul Reinsch (who was Hornbeck's instructor at the University of Wisconsin before becoming
President Wilson's envoy to China) also affected Hornbeck's perceptions
of Japan—the power which posed a constant threat to China's territorial integrity (Thomson, 1973: 82). Japan was therefore viewed by Hornbeck as an inherently aggressive entity and as the power which
represented the antithesis of Chinese values and patterns of international behavior (Pelz, 1974: 74).

This image of Japan, which remained essentially unchanged
throughout Hornbeck's long career in the State Department, was first
clearly articulated in his book *Contemporary Politics in the Far East* (1916).
Closely patterned on the distinction between "the threat of Japanese imperialism" and the "centrality and immense promise of China," the study
asserted that the United States had special "moral obligations" to help
shape China's future, while depicting Japan's "Monroe Doctrine for Asia"
(i.e., the Twenty-One Demands) as "a serious threat not only to John
Hay's Open Door doctrine but also to the Monroe Doctrine itself"
(quoted in Thomson, 1973: 89). Hornbeck was thus acutely sensitive to
the regional balance of power and repeatedly warned, as early as 1916,
that "any upsetting of the political status quo in the Far East [could] become a menace to our interests, along with those of other nations"
(quoted in Thomson, 1973: 89).

Eighteen years later this dichotomous vision of the forces operating
in the Far Eastern theater remained intact. Seeking to juxtapose the
Chinese and Japanese national modus operandi, the political affairs advisor observed in a memorandum sent to Secretary Hull on February 26,
1934:

> Generally and comparatively speaking, the Chinese have been
> and are easy-going and complacent, whereas the Japanese have
> been and are active, aggressive and inclined to be bellicose. . . .
> As a matter of fact neither China nor Japan behave at all well in

international relations. Both cause other countries a great deal
of unusual and unpleasant bother. But the Chinese delinquencies are comparatively petty and are for the most part those of
inefficiency and ineptitude, whereas the Japanese delinquencies
are on a large scale and involve important consequences and
are deliberately planned and efficiently carried out. (quoted in
Nixon, 1969: Vol. 1, 660)

During the decade preceding Pearl Harbor, these preconceived,
sharply delineated images of the Pacific precipitated (as in the case of
Stimson) certain derivative, fully congruent policy recommendations,
which were aligned with the premises of coercive diplomacy.
Hornbeck's commitment to a posture of utmost firmness as a means of
restraining Japan was evident during the Manchurian crises. Following
the initial reports of the outbreak of hostilities in Manchuria in September 1931, he immediately adopted a firm line toward Japan and
demanded that she be branded "an outlaw" by the United States (Rappaport, 1963: 58). Believing that Japan could only be deterred by hard-line
American policy, Hornbeck called for the introduction of "economic
weapons" (Rappaport, 1963: 120–121) as a means of curbing Japan's expansionist drive in Manchuria. Such a policy, he observed, could be implemented through appropriate legislation combined with the volun-
tary cooperation of American bankers and businessmen. In a
memorandum dated January 21, 1932, he proposed that American bankers refuse to grant loans to Japan pending the "development of evidence
regarding Japan's methods in handling the Manchurian problems."

Seven years later, in the aftermath of Japan's invasion of China
(which further reinforced his preliminary dichotomous vision of the
Far Eastern theater), this predilection for a determined, punitive course
toward Japan surfaced once again with much vehemence. Thus on November 14, 1938, Hornbeck drafted a memorandum entitled "The Tung
Oil Project and American Policy in General in Regard to the Far East."
Therein, this member of the hard-line coalition expressed unqualified
support for the Chinese cause, comprehensively articulating his belief
in the effectiveness of a policy comprising "diplomatic, economic and
potential military pressures":

> The American government has during recent years been oppos-
> ing Japan by use of words (appeal to principles, to rules of law,
> to provisions of treaties, etc.). Our Department of State may be
> able to get the better of the Japanese Foreign Office—though

even that is not certain—in the field of argumentation, but victories on our part in that field will *not* halt the forward march of Japan's military machine. The fact is that unless the United States expects and intends to use weapons *stronger* than those of argument, continuance on our part along that line is almost certain to lead to the development of a situation in which this country will have either to accept a diplomatic defeat or find itself forced to resort to arms. The most practicable course for us to follow would be that of giving assistance to the Chinese and *withholding* those things which are of assistance to the Japanese, toward prolonging and strengthening China's resistance and curtailing Japan's ability to continue military operations against China. If and when, however, we commit ourselves to that line of action, we should do so whole-heartedly and with determination. We should not take some one step without expecting, intending and being able to take further steps, many further steps, in the same direction. Such steps should include a combination of diplomatic, economic and potential military *pressures.* If this Government wishes to embark upon such a course, *it* should be prepared to consider seriously the taking of such steps as denunciation of the U.S.–Japan Commercial Treaty of 1911, repeal of the Neutrality Act, retaliatory tariff measures against Japan, *placing of embargoes upon trade and shipping between Japan and the United States,* [as well as] disposal of our naval resources in such manner as to indicate to the Japanese Government and nation that we "mean business." (PSF, 1938: Box 37, China: June-December; italics in original)

One month later, in a memorandum dated December 20, 1938, Hornbeck (in U.S. Department of State, 1941: Vol 4, the Far East, 425–426) once again expressed his wholehearted support for a coercive strategy in the Pacific:

I consider it highly desirable that a plan be made at this time for a comprehensive and thorough-going program of measures of material pressure which might be applied. . . . My view is that adoption of such a program, and letting it be known that the program is in existence and may be carried out, might contribute substantially toward obviating the development of a situation in which danger of armed conflict might become an actuality.

Hornbeck was fully committed to his preconceived background images and congruent policy recommendations. In connection to the Far Eastern crisis as it unfolded in 1940–1941, he had held "that the Japanese wanted to diminish the amount of aid flowing to Great Britain [and] to force the American people to stand silent and idle while Japan proceeded with her program of aggression in the Far East" (quoted in Butow, 1974: 123). In a memorandum dated February 24, 1940, Hornbeck had asserted that in light of British and French "current weakness and vulnerability in the Far East, and their inclination toward appeasing Japan, there was a need for the exercise by the U.S. of positive influence in relations with Japan, with China and with Great Britian and France" (in *The Morgenthau Diary*, 1940: Book 242, February 21–26). More specifically, in a section of the memorandum entitled "Objectives of American Policy," he recommended

> that the U.S. in no way bend itself to processes of compromise (any "Munich agreement") in or with regard to the Far East; that the U.S. refrain from any "bargaining" in connection with political matters in the Far East or in the relations of this country with Far Eastern countries; that . . . the U.S. continue [to] extend its procedures of pressure . . . which, having begun with drying up of credits, application of "moral embargo," etc., may be extended to discontinuance of most-favored treatment of exports, and, if necessary, ultimately, carefully selected and skillfully imposed embargoes on some types of exports.

A few months later, on August 17, 1940, the Japanese intensified the pressure on the Dutch East Indies for increased shipments of petroleum products. Hornbeck—who was briefed on the Batavia negotiations by Shell's representatives in the United States—reacted violently, making it clear that he "disliked concessions to the Japanese in general and this one in particular since . . . it included . . . aviation gasoline and very high octane crudes." He would not have objected to low-grade crude, but to his sensibility aviation stocks smacked of "appeasement" and he therefore had concluded that "resistance of outrageous demands was more likely to maintain peace than concessions" (quoted in Anderson, 1975: 147–148).

Thus, convinced that the "policy of pressure" which he so persistently advocated in the wake of the "Mukden incident" was the appropriate course to follow, and that "the weakness of Hoover. . . had sown the seeds of the present crisis," Hornbeck tended (like Stimson) to approach the American-Japanese crisis of 1941 in terms of the lessons which he had drawn from the "Anglo-American failure to stand up to Japan during the Manchurian episode" (quoted in Thomson, 1973: 102, from a memorandum dated October 16, 1941).

During the period preceding Pearl Harbor, these "lessons of the past" (May, 1973a)—the result of Hornbeck's personal experiences—were fully incorporated into a dichotomous worldview which was predicated upon the conviction that "the only thing that really impresses and tends to restrain the Japanese at this point is evidence of assessed capacity and intention" (quoted in Thomson, 1973: 102–103, from a memorandum which Hornbeck sent to Sumner Welles on August 18, 1941). Hornbeck believed that war in the Pacific would be avoided as long as the United States maintained "a bold and positive" policy, and in April 1941 observed that he "did not for one moment believe that the real authorities in Japan, whoever they might be, would embark upon war in the southwestern Pacific because of lack of success in a 'negotiation' with the United States in the near future" (quoted in Butow, 1974: 155; see also Emmerson, 1978: 117). Similarly, in a memorandum dated July 16, 1941, Hornbeck strongly recommended the freezing of Japanese assets in the United States, and in August—following the "freezing order" of July 25—argued for additional coercive measures inluding "a new show of force in the Western Pacific" and the immediate deployment of additional planes to Manila (quoted in Thomson, 1973: 102–103).

Three months later, in November, John K. Emmerson (a junior embassy officer in Tokyo) visited Washington, warning that Japan might "go to war in desperation" (Emmerson, 1978: 117). He was rebuked by Hornbeck, who stated (Emmerson, 1978: 117; see also Thomson, 1973: 101): "Name me one country in history which ever went to war in desperation." This optimism remained unshattered as late as November 27, 1941 (i.e., less than two weeks before the Pearl Harbor attack), when Hornbeck observed that:

> The Japanese Government does not desire or intend or expect to have forthwith [an] armed conflict with the United States. . . . My bets are five to one that the United States and Japan will not be at "war" on or before December 15, three to one against war by January 15, and "even money" against war by March 1. . . . stated briefly, the undersigned does not believe that this country is now on the immediate verge of "war" in the Pacific. (quoted in Thomson, 1973: 103–104)

STIMSON, MORGENTHAU, AND HORNBECK:
IN PURSUIT OF COERCIVE DIPLOMACY

The preceding analysis has sought to demonstrate that in the thinking
of Stimson, Morgenthau, and Hornbeck, certain lessons of the past
(which were drawn as a result of personal experiences in such events as
the Manchurian crisis) were integrated into dichotomous, sharply delineated worldviews. These members of the Roosevelt policy elite were
predisposed to see world politics as conflict-ridden and to perceive *any*
opponent (including Japan) as inherently aggressive. Thus they clearly
represent the "hard-line" type of political actor (Snyder and Diesing,
1977: 298). Committed to the notion that the adversary—perceived as a
monolithic entity—is pursuing virtually unlimited expansionist objectives, this type of policy maker therefore tends to advocate irreconcila-
bility as the optimal way of deterring the opponent (Luard, 1967: 171, 177;
Morgan, 1977: 154–155; Snyder and Diesing, 1977: 298–299). In the case
of the Roosevelt policy machine, it was this hard-line approach which
ultimately became the source of the official American posture in the Pacific.

By the eve of Pearl Harbor, Secretaries Stimson and Morgenthau—the
leaders of the hard-line coalition—succeeded in inducing both Secretary
Hull and President Roosevelt to set aside their initial reservations and
thus to give support to the coercive strategy which they had advocated
so persistently. With the remaining members of the "blocking coalition" (which had sought to frustrate or delay at least some of the punitive measures supported by the hard-liners) reduced to impotence, this
"majority coalition" could proceed apace toward the unmitigated implementation of its strategy. Even Admiral Stark's memorandum (warning
against economic sanctions) to the president, dated July 21, 1941, could
not stem the tide of the unfolding American strategy.

This nonconciliatory tendency culminated on July 25, 1941, when
President Roosevelt decided to freeze all Japanese assets in the United
States in economic retaliation for Japan's occupation of naval and air
bases in southern Indochina. This "freezing order" enabled Morgenthau
and his department to implement their long-standing plan to embargo
all exports to Japan and was supported by Secretary Hull, who was particularly incensed by the Japanese move.[2] The political culmination of
this process was Roosevelt's acceptance of the uncompromising Ten
Point Plan, which led to the final breakdown of American-Japanese
negotiations.

Immensely pleased by this "freezing order," Stimson and Morgenthau were uninhibited in their telephone conversation of August 9, 1941 (Stimson's *Diary*, 1941: Vol. 35, August 1–October 31), in which they set out to coordinate their future actions regarding the Japanese:

STIMSON: Now, I've—you're the only man with whom I've ever held four parleys on this subject, and so I take it up with you. . . . The one interest—one thing that I know that I am interested in and that I know anything about . . . is the subject of our old relations to Japan and the embargo. . . . And you saw eye-to-eye with me on that.

MORGENTHAU: I did on that and many other things.

STIMSON: [Japan, at that time, was] rattled and scared. . . . there have been gentle afternoon teas going on between our State Department and their Ambassador. . . . Under the impulse of the Japanese move to the south, we sent an ultimatum in regard to Thailand. . . . And showed a stiffening up rather than an amelioration of the tea parties.

MORGENTHAU: I agree with you.

STIMSON: But now I hope that they're not going to start off with any more relaxation with Japan.

MORGENTHAU: Oh, no.

STIMSON: But will just keep her right up to the bit.

MORGENTHAU: . . . I can assure you that from our standpoint there won't be any stiffening, because my attitude is just—

STIMSON: Any unstiffening.

MORGENTHAU: No, no. We'll stay right where we are. Because for two years we've wanted to freeze their assets and stop buying their silk and all that sort of thing. And on the economic front, I think the thing that we did that had the greatest repercussion is when we tied up their money.

STIMSON: I think it did, too.

MORGENTHAU: But when we tied up their money, then that got them financially where they could take it the least.

STIMSON: You froze their assets.

MORGENTHAU: And that settled the question about their getting oil, because they had no money to buy any oil . . . and from that day to this, they haven't bought any gasoline.

As this conversation clearly indicates, the two "coalition builders" were quick to recognize that their success in the interdepartmental debate over the shaping of American diplomacy in the Pacific was the product of their unity, resolve, and skill in utilizing certain administrative resources, enabling them to translate their pre-existing images of the Japanese opponent into derivative action.

In early November 1941, both Stimson and Morgenthau, once again acting in cooperation, staunchly opposed Roosevelt's last-ditch effort to deviate even momentarily from the parameters of the hard-line posture, which by then had become the official American policy in the Pacific; and to conclude a modus vivendi agreement with Japan. Stimson's conviction that Japan would not honor any agreement was coupled with his belief that a "truce" with Japan would only damage American prestige because it would entail abandonment of the "fundamental principles on which we had stood for so long." Thus, on November 6, upon learning from the president the details of the modus vivendi proposal, Stimson strongly objected, maintaining that "the Chinese would feel that any such agreement was a desertion of them" (Stimson's *Diary*, 1941: Vol. 36, November 1–December 31, 1941).

In his disapproval of the modus vivendi proposal, Stimson was once again joined by his coalition partner Morgenthau, who drafted a personal letter to the president (Morgenthau's *Presidential Diaries*, 1941: Book 4, March 1–December 31). The letter was never sent, as Roosevelt had subsequently abandoned his own proposal and instead accepted the White memorandum, which was submitted on November 18, 1941, by Morgenthau to Roosevelt and Hull and which constituted the basis of Hull's uncompromising Ten Point Plan. It is nonetheless appropriate to quote from this letter, as it clearly sets forth Morgenthau's perspective on the Far East:

> Mr. President, I want to explain in language as strong as I can command, my feeling that the need is for iron firmness. No settlement with Japan that in any way seems to the American people, or to the rest of the world, to be a retreat, no matter how temporary, from our increasingly clear policy of opposition to aggressors, will be viewed as consistent with the position of our government or with the leadership that you have established. Certainly the independence of the millions of brave people in China, who have been carrying on their fight for four long, hard years against Japanese aggression is of no less concern to us and to the world than the independence of Thailand or French Indo-

China. No matter what explanation is offered to the Public of a "truce" with Japan, the American people, the Chinese people, and the oppressed peoples of Europe, as well as those forces in Britain and in Russia who are with us in this fight, will regard it as a confession of American weakness, and vacillation. How else can the world possibly interpret a relaxation of the economic pressure . . . when that relaxation is undertaken not because Japan has actually abandoned it, but only because she promises not to extend her aggressive acts to other countries? The parallel with Munich is inescapable.

After 1936, Stimson, Morgenthau, and Hornbeck increasingly expected that in the long run the United States would inevitably be dragged into the European conflict. Nevertheless, until the very eve of war they upheld the belief that despite her association with the Axis powers, Japan could still be deterred by a "firm and positive" policy. However, the means they had chosen to achieve their objective of maintaining peace contributed, in the final analysis, to the outbreak of hostilities in the Pacific (Graebner, 1973: 45–46, 51).

AN APPRAISAL

The pursuit of an effective, coercive strategy, observe George, Hall, and Simons (1981: 25), depends upon an optimal mix or trade-off between threats and positive inducements. They assert that such a combination may well provide the impetus for a settlement by reducing the opponent's disinclination to comply with what is demanded of him:

> Coercive diplomacy in any given situation may be facilitated by, if indeed it does not require, genuine concessions to an opponent as part of a quid pro quo that secures one's essential demands. Coercive diplomacy, therefore, needs to be distinguished from pure coercion, it includes the possibility of bargains, negotiations, and compromises as well as coercive threats. What the stick cannot achieve by itself, unless it is a very formidable one, can possibly be achieved by combining a carrot with a stick. (p. 26)

Turning now from the abstract context of bargaining theory to the more tangible framework of American-Japanese relations as they developed in 1940 and 1941, it is clear that Stimson, Morgenthau, and Hornbeck recommended in general the "try and see" variant of coercive diplomacy, insisting that the imposition of a series of increasingly escalating economic sanctions would ultimately serve as the most effective deterrent against Japanese military aggression. However, this conviction and its corollary—that faced with a firm U.S. policy, Japan would act in a rational, prudent, and responsible manner—ultimately proved to be mistaken (Janis, 1972: 76; Jervis, 1979: 300–301).

True, the policy of economic sanctions against Japan occasionally produced the desired outcome predicted by Stimson and Morgenthau. For example, after Japan's assets in the United States were frozen (on July 25, 1941), Japan did demonstrate an eagerness for compromise, appearing to have abandoned certain plans for further expansion which had been decided upon only a short while before (Tsou, 1963: 29; Pratt, 1964: 419–420; Hosoya, 1968: 110). However, since there was no simultaneous attempt to conciliate Japan on crucial issues, American coercive policy was doomed to failure (Schroeder, 1958: 88–89; Hosoya, 1968: 110; George, Hall, and Simons, 1971: 245–246; Jervis, 1979: 300–305). Indeed, the Stimson-Morgenthau formula for "firmness and boldness," when translated into an inflexible policy of severe economic sanctions (which as such was devoid of any positive inducements), ultimately contributed to the outbreak of the Pacific War.

Although the costs of launching a military campaign against the United States were perceived by the Japanese as high (relative to the prospective benefits) this did not deter them from ultimately challenging the satus quo (George, Hall, and Simons, 1971: 245; Lauren, 1979: 192; Betts, 1982: 134–135). It is therefore clear in retrospect that the powerful coalition of hard-line policy makers "failed to formulate a carrot and stick that sufficed to overcome the strong unwillingness of the Japanese government to accept demands to curtail its aggressive activities in Asia" (George, Hall, and Simons, 1971: 246).

Furthermore, even on those occasions (as during August 1941) when the Japanese government did demonstrate an eagerness to compromise and abandon some of its plans for further expansion (Hosoya, 1973: 161), the "bold and positive" American policy continued to foster militancy among the influential middle-echelon officers within the Japanese General Staff. This trend was at first unobtrusive, but it grew more salient and influential as it became increasingly clear that Japanese moderation did not inspire the United States to reciprocate (Morgan, 1977: 195).

Ultimately, when confronted with an irreconcilable, coercive drive, "a desperate Japanese government chose the desperate, low-confidence strategy of war with the United States" (George, Hall, and Simons, 1971: 246).

An example of the pattern of Japanese reaction to American firmness is provided by the events following the decision of July 26, 1940, to impose an embargo on shipments of scrap iron, aviation fuel, and lubricants to Japan. The imposition of these economic sanctions clearly did not prompt the Japanese army to adopt a more moderate posture toward the United States. On the contrary, the military, which had played an influential role in the Japanese policy-making process throughout the period preceding the war, advocated strong retaliatory measures. The secret war diary of the Japanese General Staff (Hosoya, 1968: 107) reveals that on August 2, 1940, a proposal advocating "steps to be taken against the U.S. embargo" was drafted within the General Staff. At the same time, the first section of the Japanese Naval General Staff drew up a "study relating to policy towards French Indochina," which advocated "strengthening" Japanese southern policy as a response to the pressure of economic sanctions. In this document (Hosoya, 1968: 107–108: Sadao, 1973: 251) the possibility was considered that caught between her planned advanced into French Indochina and the imposition of severe American economic sanctions, Japan would have to face "a situation in which it would have no choice but to stiffen its determination and invade the Dutch Indies in order to obtain oil fields." The navy in particular was dependent on fuel oil; and since trade with the United States was endangered by the increasingly coercive economic policy pursued by the Roosevelt administration, Japanese naval officers felt that they had no other option but to advance southward in quest of alternative sources of oil (Sadao, 1973: 246–256; Tsunoda, 1980: 243). Later, when the total embargo on Japanese trade went into effect on August 1, 1941, Japan was confronted with an oil shortage that precipitated military action designed, in the words of the Navy General Staff chief Admiral Asami Nagano "to break the iron fetters strangling Japan" (quoted in Sadao, 1973: 254).

Evidently, then, the imposition of economic sanctions only strengthened the determination of influential segments of the Japanese defense forces (which perceived the alternative to fighting as permitting a drastic erosion of positions already established) to resist American economic pressure despite the risks involved, and to demand executing their plan for a southern expansion (Sadao, 1973: 253; Tsunoda, 1980: 255, 258; Lebow, 1981: 195; Jervis, 1982–83: 13). Nor is the psychological element to be overlooked. As Hosoya (1968: 108) points out, by challenging the United States in the Pacific, the military sought to prove that Japan "was not the nation to undergo humiliation and to helplessly submit to pressures and sanctions."

Maintaining that "if Japan faced national ruin whether it decided to fight the United States or to submit to America's demands, it must choose to fight," Navy chief Nagano asserted, in his statement at the crucial Imperial Conference of September 6, 1941, that he would rather go down fighting than surrender without a struggle—for a surrender would spell "spiritual as well as physical destruction for the nation" (quoted in Sadao, 1973: 254; see also Jervis, 1982–83: 13; Thies, 1980: 263, 400). American statesmen seemed to be incapable of understanding the ways in which their opponent tended to see the world and underestimated the value placed by the Japanese military on prevailing will (George and Smoke, 1974: 582–583; Jervis, 1979: 306; Lauren, 1979: 190–192; Betts, 1982: 122–125, 128, 138–140).[3]

The pressures exerted by the army and navy further increased in September 1940 following the deadlock in the negotiations between Japan and the Dutch East Indies. Concurrently, Japan was experiencing difficulties in her political negotiations with Indochina over Japanese troop movements and airport facilities in northern Indochina. Reacting to these events and pressures, the Japanese government decided on September 13, 1940, to accept the General Staff's proposal and to issue an ultimatum to the Vichy government, which ruled Indochina. This ultimatum demanded the immediate conclusion of a military agreement which had granted permission for the passage of Japanese troops through the Tonkin region and the use of airport facilities in northern Indochina. Less than a year later, on July 12, 1941, pressure was once again exerted on the Vichy government when Japan demanded air and naval bases in *southern* Indochina and the right to station an unspecified number of air, sea, and ground forces there.

The demands raised by the General Staff in 1940 and 1941 were not always acceptable to the Japanese government. However, even when the army's recommendations of a strong retaliatory policy against the United States were not immediately implemented, its point of view remained a constant source of pressure both within and outside the government. While the army was not altogether opposed to negotiations with the United States, it insisted on limiting their scope. Eventually, following the unyielding American response to indications of Japan's readiness to compromise (e.g., Hull's Ten Point Plan), the views of the military faction gained influence and became an even greater determining factor in the formulation of Japanese foreign policy.

Thus, the convictions held so firmly by Stimson, Morgenthau, and Hornbeck proved erroneous. Assuming that intensive economic pressure would under all circumstances succeed in moderating Japanese attitudes and policies, they failed to properly evaluate the risks inherent in such a posture (Janis, 1972: 76; Iriye, 1981: 20; Jervis, 1982–83: 23).[4]

These policy makers were so committed to their preconceptions that they remained oblivious to the warnings of the War Plans Division, which strongly opposed the freezing of all Japanese assets in the United States. Ten days before the order was issued the Division had warned (Neumann, 1957: 154) that an embargo on Japan would "possibly . . . involve the U.S. in [an] early war in the Pacific." Several months later, on October 2, 1941, Colonel Hayes A. Kroner, acting assistant chief of staff of the American armed forces, pointed out (U.S. Congress, Pearl Harbor *Hearings*, 1946: Part 14, 1358; Schroeder, 1958: 178–179) that any demand that the Japanese evacuate their troops from China forthwith was impossible for Japan to meet. Kroner concluded that "we must cease at once our attempt to bring about the withdrawal of Japanese armed forces from China."

But the American hard-liners could not accommodate their basic beliefs to accept these views. They were incapable of recognizing the fragility of the moderate forces operating on Japan's political scene and were predisposed to view the Japanese opponent as more hostile, homogeneous, and disciplined than it was in reality (see, in this connection, Thies, 1980: 322, 360–363).

The rigidity of Stimson and his colleagues similarly prevented them from seriously considering the views of Joseph C. Grew, the American ambassador to Tokyo, who sought to make them aware of the dynamics of Japan's political, military, and social structures. The hard-liners were oblivious to the spate of messages he sent which warned against assuming that continuing economic sanctions would automatically force Japan to adopt a restrained policy toward the United States and which emphasized that the Japanese temperament could not be measured by American standards of logic (Jervis, 1982–83: 4). They remained convinced that the Japanese decision as to whether or not to wage war would be based primarily on cost-benefit military calculations rather than on nationalistic, ideological, or psychological grounds (Luard, 1967: 177; Ben-Zvi, 1976: 384–385, 1980: 96–100; Thies, 1980: 400; Betts, 1982: 134). Moreover, thinking chiefly in political terms, they failed to recognize the important role played in the decision-making process by the middle-echelon, militant Japanese officers. As Hosoya (1968: 112) points out, "They overlooked the fact that in their way of thinking and behaving, the middle-echelon group somewhat differed from the upper echelon. . . . They were more adventuristic, contemptible [*sic*] of compromise and militarily-minded" (see also Betts, 1982: 137).

By asserting that the Japanese would recognize the disparity in strength favoring the United States and would therefore decide against war, the hard-liners were, in fact, applying to Japan a Western model of the decision-making process and a Western concept of rational behavior, predicated upon the notion of logical positivism (see, in this connection, Pipes, 1981: 77; Jervis, 1982–83: 14). They ignored the possibility that Japanese concepts and patterns of behavior might not fit their frame of reference. They viewed Asia "as no different from other parts of the world, where the rules of moral conduct equally applied," and failed to perceive the Japanese predisposition to make high-risk decisions at crucial moments (Jones, 1954: 461; Knorr, 1964: 462–463; Hosoya, 1968: 112, 1974: 355–359; George, Hall and Simons, 1971: 246; Morgan, 1977: 154; Betts, 1978: 83–84, 1982: 122; Jervis, 1979: 296–307; Thies, 1980: 400). Thus, although provided with a plethora of reliable intelligence indicators (including the deciphered messages of "Magic," the top-secret Japanese diplomatic code), which in November warned that war between Japan and the United States (or Britain) was imminent, the hard-liners remained committed, almost to the very end, to their belief that Japan would not dare to challenge the United States directly in the Pacific (Wohlstetter, 1962; Kahn, 1973; Ben-Zvi, 1976: 384–385, 389–390; Jervis, 1979: 300–301, 1982–83: 7, 13; Iriye, 1981: 22 passim). As Betts (1982: 134) concludes:

> Conventional notions of deterrence assume that nations will sacrifice more to prevent losses than to achieve gains, and thus that aggressors will not risk as much as those who aim to preserve the status quo. Even if true, the problem in 1941 was that U.S. authorities did not appreciate how the Japanese believed that continuing the status quo would constitute a loss rather than just the absence of gain; they did not discuss Japan's despair about "gradual exhaustion," encirclement, strangulation, and defeat. Outside the embassy in Tokyo, U.S. leaders were insensitive to the quasi-religious impetus behind Japanese imperialism. (see also Jervis, 1982–83: 13).

Similarly, by relying on such analogies as "appeasement" and "Munich," which were insensitively transplanted to the context of American-Japanese relations, the hard-liners failed to recognize the many differences in context and background which separated past events from the occurrences of 1940 and 1941 (Blum, 1970: 212; for general analyses of the dangers inherent in analogical thinking see Hoffmann, 1968: 137; May, 1973: passim; Jervis, 1976: 218–222, 228–229, 264–276, 1982–83: 21).

As indicated, American policy toward Japan was rooted in and motivated by a deep feeling of suspicion toward that nation. This emotional bias was an important element in a worldview which divided the globe in a simplistic and generalized manner into two opposing camps: the fascist-aggressive nations, including Japan, Germany, and Italy, which always acted in close collaboration and were completely united in their ultimate intentions; and the peace-loving nations, including the United States and China (Neumann, 1963: 267).

Notwithstanding that the Japanese-German alliance—the Tripartite Pact of September 27, 1940—"was ineffective from the start" (Meskill, 1966: 4; see also Friedländer, 1967: passim), the hard-liners remained fully convinced that they faced a united revisionist front seeking to disrupt the global balance of power (Schroeder, 1958: 103; Iriye, 1967: 202; Russett, 1972: 21; Ben-Zvi, 1975: passim; Morley, 1976: 182). Indeed, although the main Japanese objective in concluding the Tripartite Pact was to deter the United States from interfering in its southern drive by presenting an *appearance* of a formidable German-Japanese military combination (without actually committing Tokyo to any self-enforcing, automatic framework of military cooperation with the Axis powers [Hosoya, 1976: 245–256]), the architects of American diplomacy in the Pacific continued to adhere to their preconceived, dichotomous visions of the world. In the words of Stanley Hornbeck

> We should keep in mind the fact that for all practical purposes the world's great powers are today divided into two camps: on the one side are three aggressor nations—in combination: Japan, Germany and Italy; on the other side are China, Great Britain—and the United States. . . . The conflict which is raging today is between two great groups of major powers, is between two ideologies, is between those nations . . . which wish to hold and those nations which are out to "take"—and this conflict is world-wide. . . . Whatever *any* one of the to-have-and-to-hold group loses is a loss for *all* members of the group; and whatever any one of the "take" group gains is a gain for all members of

that group. (U.S. Congress, Pearl Harbor *Hearings*, 1946: Part 14, 1947, 1993; italics in original)

Contrary to Hornbeck's perceptions, the association with Germany by no means required Japan to relinquish her independence of decision and action. In a "personal letter" from the German ambassador to Japan, Eugene Ott, to the Japanese foreign minister, Yosuke Matsuoka, which was attached to the Tripartite Pact, it was agreed that "the respective governments" would determine for themselves whether aggression had occurred and whether they were obliged to intervene (Meskill, 1966: 19). In sharp contrast with the apparent implication of Article 3 of the treaty, which obliged Japan "to assist with all political, economic, and military means" should Germany or Italy be attacked by a new belligerent, such as the United States or the Soviet Union, the letter agreed to reserve for Japan "the freedom to decide for itself whether an 'attack' had taken place" (Hosoya, 1976: 253–254). Furthermore, not only were the policies which Japan and Germany pursued respectively toward the United States essentially uncoordinated in the aftermath of the Tripartite Pact, but—toward the end of 1941—relations between the two partners became even more strained as Japan repeatedly demonstrated a marked coolness toward the Axis, treating the Tripartite Pact as a dead letter. The conclusion, on April 13, 1941, of a neutrality pact between Japan and the Soviet Union (in defiance of German expectations), the initiation of Operation Barbarossa which surprised and dismayed Tokyo, and Japan's determination to proceed with the Hull-Nomura conversations regardless of Germany's strong opposition (and without even informing her of various proposals and developments arising in their course) are but a few illustrations of the cleavage and disunity which clouded the scene of American-Japanese relations in 1941. In Meskill's words (1966: 4):

> The conclusion of the Tripartite Pact itself and the first fifteen months of the pact [September 1940 to December 1941] proved that in the crucial area of political and military coordination, what then seemed to the outside world like the establishment of a common conspiracy against the peace was merely a fortuitous meeting of two lines of force, criss-crossing in the pursuit of different objectives. These lines intersected only twice, once in September 1940, when the Tripartite Pact was concluded, and again in December 1941, when Japan and Germany within three days of each other declared war on the United States. Before, between

and after these dates, the allies aimed at different and often incompatible ends, often deceiving each other and themselves into
the bargain. (see also Hosoya, 1976: 253–255)

As it was incapable of convincing Japan to coordinate her U.S. policy
with Germany, the German foreign ministry could only hope that the
United States would somehow avoid deepening the wedge between the
two Axis partners. This hope was frequently expressed by the German
ambassador to Japan, Eugene Ott. For example, in a memorandum to
Foreign Minister Ribbentrop which Ott sent on July 10, 1941, the ambassador observed (quoted in Friedländer, 1967: 273): "The attempts of the
Anglophiles [in Tokyo] to find a compromise [with the U.S.] are, I think,
doomed to failure in view of the American attitude." And on August 22,
1941, Ott similarly reported:

> As in the earlier crises it is to be expected now, too, that friends
> of American Anglophile circles will try . . . to bring about a
> compromise with America and thoroughly eliminate the night-
> mare of encirclement. . . . In view of America's unwillingness to
> compromise . . . which has always prevented an understanding
> heretofore . . . such attempts cannot succeed.

Ultimately, these hopes and expectations indeed materialized as the
last-ditch effort to reach a modus vivendi agreement between the United
States and Japan proved abortive. True, not all the developments which
strained Japanese-German relations were known at the time to American policy makers. Some, however, were clearly identified by Ambassador Grew and his staff, and by several strategic planners in the General
Staff. In numerous memoranda (compiled during the period immediately following the conclusion of the Tripartite Pact, as well as in
the aftermath of the German attack on the Soviet Union) they repeatedly stressed that relations among the Tripartite partners were tense;
and that Japan had indicated her readiness to withdraw de facto from
the Tripartite Pact and to ignore all her obligations to her partners in
order to further an agreement with the United States.

For example, in a telegram dispatched by Grew to Hull on October 2,
1940, one week after the conclusion of the Tripartite Pact, the ambassador pointed out:

Our observations since the signing of the pact point to a marked lack of enthusiasm on the part of a large element of Japanese public opinion, both in certain military and in some civilian and government circles. It is commonly believed by competent foreign observers that the Navy, which was not associated with the negotiation of the pact and whose officers were conspicuously absent from the various official functions held in celebration of the signing of the Pact, is not only unenthusiastic, but perhaps opposed to the present orientation of affairs. It is also held by certain observers that the Premier himself was forced to accept the pact contrary to his wishes. (U.S. Department of State, 1943: Vol. 1, General: 657)

Similarly, in the wake of the German onslaught on the Soviet Union, Grew informed Hull in a number of messages (U.S. Department of State, 1943: Vol. 4, The Far East, 187) that the "new war, far from inspiring harmony among the Tripartite allies, was causing surprise and dismay in Tokyo, and that consequently there were increasing signs of Tripartite disunity and of a mounting Japanese determination to pursue an independent course of action vis-à-vis its Axis partners." As he wrote to the secretary of state in a typical message from June 26, 1941, "An unusually well-informed Japanese remarked today to us that Japan's policy of cooperation with the Axis powers had been predicated on continued close association between Germany and Soviet Russia and that the breaking out of war between these two countries had destroyed the fundamental basis of Japan's pro-Axis policy."

On the very same day, Naval Attaché Creswell reported from Tokyo to the office of the chief of naval operations, Navy Department (in Hopkins, 1935–45: Military Intelligence Reports, Far Eastern Documents, Box 193) that "the outbreak of hostilities between Germany and Russia has been a great shock to Japan." A concurrent report from the Far Eastern theater, which was sent on June 25, 1941, by Major F. P. Munson, assistant military attaché in China, to the Military Intelligence Division in the War Department's General Staff (Hopkins, 1935–45: Military Intelligence Reports, Far Eastern Documents, Box 193) went even further, maintaining that "with the sudden outbreak of war between Germany and the Soviet Union, there has been a subtle change in the . . . attitude of Japan toward the United States. . . . This is the second time in two years [the message added] that Germany has 'double-crossed' Japan and the Japanese must realize that if their Axis partners turn against them they are certainly without another friend in the world."

One month later, in the wake of the establishment in Tokyo of Prince Konoye's second cabinet, the field evaluations became even more emphatic, predicting a rupture in Japanese-German relations. For example, in an intelligence report compiled on July 29, 1941, Naval Attaché Creswell asserted that

> in foreign affairs, it is expected that [the new government] will follow an increasingly independent course in order to settle the China Incident and consolidate her position on the continent before the European war is ended. *While it is unlikely that she will break openly with Berlin and Rome, her policies will probably be independent of the Axis powers, since she has learned that they are not to be trusted.* (PSF, 1940–1941: Box 200: Probability of an Outbreak of War: Documents N: Naval Attaché Tokyo: Vol. 2: January 16, 1940–September 22, 1941, italics added)

For all their significance, none of these developments was fully perceived by Stimson, Morgenthau, and Hornbeck. Adhering to their preconceived, immutable images of Japan, they failed to recognize the fluctuations that characterized the Japanese domestic scene during the period preceding Pearl Harbor (see, in this connection, De Santis, 1980: 206). Hence, they remained totally unresponsive to the factions in Japan which opposed war with the United States and were oblivious to the possibility that conciliatory American moves (such as the relaxation of the embargo imposed on shipments of scrap iron, oil, and other materials to Japan) could well strengthen these groups' relative position vis-à-vis their powerful opponents in Tokyo, who argued that war with the United States was inevitable (Ben-Zvi, 1975: 244).

The hard-liners also tended, on the basis of their fixed background images, to diagnose and interpret specific developments involving Japan in a manner reinforcing their belief systems. For example, Stimson, whose threat assessments were derived from his general skepticism regarding Japan's intentions, viewed the arrival in Washington (in November 1941) of the Japanese diplomat Saburo Kurusu as evidence of a hardening in Japan's position and as a prelude to the presentation of unacceptable proposals. Kurusu was perceived as an enthusiastic supporter of the Japanese-German rapprochement and as a diplomat not to be trusted. "Kurusu was described as a deceitful man, having neither an appearance nor an attitude that commanded confidence or respect" (quoted in Hsu, 1952: 301; Butow, 1961: 242–243).

It is symptomatic that even Kurusu's appearance was allowed by Stimson to influence his perceptions of Japanese intentions. Moreover, Stimson's evaluation of Kurusu's mission was insufficiently supported even by the factual evidence available at the time. True, Kurusu was the Japanese ambassador in Berlin in September 1940, when the Tripartite Pact was concluded. However, that he signed the pact on behalf of Japan by no means indicated that he was the architect of the Japanese-German rapprochement (as claimed by Stimson) or that he was insincere in his negotiations in Washington. None of these assumptions was in fact true. The evidence indicates that Kurusu was bypassed in the course of the negotiations leading up to the Tripartite Pact, which were conducted in Tokyo between Foreign Minister Yosuke Matsuoka and the special German envoy, Heinrich Stahmer. In addition, Kurusu did not even support the Japanese-German treaty, partly because he disagreed with its provisions and partly because he felt insulted at being excluded from the negotiations. The evidence further indicates (Hsu, 1952: 303–304) that Kurusu, an experienced, professional diplomat, was sent to the United States to assist Ambassador Nomura (who was not a professional diplomat) in an effort "to break the deadlock . . . and to bring the [Japanese-American] negotiations speedily to a successful conclusion." Moreover, it is apparent that Kurusu did his utmost to promote American-Japanese relations; and in his eagerness to engender a rapprochement with the United States, he occasionally even exceeded his instructions from Tokyo.

This evidence was not available to Stimson in its entirety at the time he made his observation, but Kurusu's public statements in Berlin seem to justify Grew's conclusion (quoted in Hsu, 1952: 303) that on the whole, Kurusu was "no more friendly to the Nazis than to us." In any event, no proof was found among the numerous Japanese messages and documents (which were intercepted before the war or captured later) to indicate either that Kurusu was insincere in his negotiations or that the Japanese government had deceitful motives for his mission. In the words of Butow (1974: 346), who reconstructed in great detail the various diplomatic initiatives and negotiations (official and non-official) which sought to avert a conflagration in the Pacific, "No evidence has come to light to cast doubt upon the Admiral's [Nomura's] insistence that the war plans of his nation were never disclosed to him, nor is there any reason to believe that his colleague, Special Envoy Saburo Kurusu, knew anything more than that war with the United States was a distinct possibility."

Also, according to a memorandum (PSF, 1941) written by Ferdinand L. Mayer (an official in the State Department who conversed with Kurusu shortly after the news of the Japanese attack became known in Washington), the Japanese diplomat seemed "quite overwhelmed and in the deepest sort of despair, both by the tone of his voice and his expression of keenest disappointment [and] his voice sounded like that of a broken man." Indeed, Mayer maintains in his memorandum of December 7 that his contact with the Japanese envoy at the time led him to believe that "Kurusu had not been informed in advance of the decision to attack."

Thus, in the absence of conclusive evidence regarding the true nature of Kurusu's mission and role, Stimson interpreted the mission in a way which reinforced his pre-existing images. He focused only on those factors which seemed to establish Kurusu's ties with Nazi Germany, such as Kurusu's mission to Berlin and ignored those which might have indicated a different impression, such as that Kurusu had served in the Japanese consular service in the United States, and that his wife was American. In Wohlstetter's terminology (1962: 3), in the absence of conclusive, unequivocal, and clear "signals" regarding the true nature of Kurusu's mission and role, Stimson was predisposed to assimilate only those bits of evidence (which proved to be part of the misleading screen of "noise") which corresponded with his worldview. Indeed, Stimson's general image of the Japanese opponent as fundamentally hostile to the United States encouraged him to define "situations of interaction" with that adversary as threatening. Consequently, ambiguous information about Kurusu was generally interpreted by him as evidence of hostility (see, in this connection, Jervis, 1976: 143–172, 1982–83: 24–28; Snyder and Diesing, 1977: 330–335; George, 1979a: 102).

The hard-liners' misinterpretation of unfolding events by no means reflected a deliberate intention to provoke Japan into an attack. As already indicated, the policy advocated by Stimson and Morgenthau had one major objective: to restrain Japan and thereby prevent war in the Pacific. Nor were Stimson and Morgenthau acting in a political or social vacuum. Their views concerning Japan were not significantly different from those held by many influential American writers, politicians, and newspapermen. As Schroeder (1958: 106) points out, a policy aimed at a relaxation of the pressures exerted on Japan would have been highly unpopular in the United States because "over the course of a decade, the American people had built up a profound hatred and distrust of Japan. When the time came that the U.S. could put heavy pressure on the Japanese, it was the moment the public had long awaited. Virtually no one wanted the pressure relaxed." The hard-liners' views thus accurately reflected the mood of a large segment of the American public, which exerted a powerful constraint on the administration's latitude of choice in approaching the Pacific predicament of 1940–1941.

In conclusion, Stimson, Morgenthau, and Hornbeck were doctrinaire in their convictions, and were unwilling to consider new evidence or any view that differed from their own—even when the different views were vehemently expressed by such an experienced diplomat as the American ambassador to Tokyo, Joseph C. Grew, and by such military strategists and intelligence officers as Brigadier-General Leonard Gerow and Admiral Stark. Moreover, whereas other policy makers (including President Roosevelt) "did not know from the very start what the crisis [was] about" and what "the opponent's specific aims and preferences [were]," Stimson and Morgenthau "knew" from the onset of the Far Eastern crisis what the Japanese were up to (quoted in Snyder and Diesing, 1977: 331–332).

The hard-liners were convinced that there was only one possible strategy to follow and approached the protracted crisis in American-Japanese relations solely in terms of their pre-existing images and in defiance of any discrepant information. Their fallacies and errors notwithstanding, these policy makers' private diaries, as well as other contemporary evidence, strongly indicate that they were all motivated by a sincere desire to avoid war in the Pacific. Unfortunately, they were to witness the futility of their policies; and ironically, in the final analysis the means they had chosen to achieve their objective of maintaining the peace contributed to the outbreak of hostilities.

NOTES

1. This analysis was closely patterned on Ben-Zvi (1975: 231–233).

2. The "freezing order" of July 25, 1941, was a retaliatory measure against Japan's moves in southern Indochina. On July 12, 1941, Japan posed an ultimatum to the Vichy government (which controlled the territory), demanding air and naval bases as well as the right to station an unspecified number of air, sea, and ground forces there. On July 21 the Vichy government yielded to the pressure and within a few days, Japanese forces entered Saigon (Schroeder, 1958: 175–177; Tsou, 1963: 29; Hosoya, 1968: 110).

3. Some of Japan's policy makers were similarly incapable of understanding how the United States perceived the unfolding crisis in the Pacific. As Jervis (1982–1983: 7) points out, "The Japanese had no doubt that the United

States would fight if they attacked Pearl Harbor. But many of Japan's leaders thought that the stakes for the U.S. were not sufficiently high to justify an all-out effort and that the Americans would instead fight a limited war, and being unable to prevail at that level of violence, would agree to a settlement which would give Japan control of east Asia" (see also Betts, 1982: 134).

4. A similar miscalculation as to the opponent's reaction was made by Foreign Minister Matsuoka, who expected the Tripartite Pact between Japan, Germany, and Italy to soften the American hard line toward Japan. According to Matsuoka's thinking, the pact was concluded in order to deter the United States and frustrate its intention to intervene against Japan's southern advance (Hosoya, 1968: 109–110). Matsuoka strongly believed that the Tripartite Pact would prevent war between Japan and America because "only by presenting a determined stand would America be deterred from entering the war against Japan" (Iriye, 1967: 209). These expectations were most clearly articulated on September 19, 1940, when, addressing the Imperial Conference, Matsuoka stated:

> Japanese-American relations have now deteriorated to the point where no improvement can be expected through courtesy or a desire for friendship. I rather fear such a weak attitude on Japan's part may only aggravate things. All we can do to improve the situation even a little, or to prevent its further aggravation, is to stand firm. . . . America's attitude toward Japan has deteriorated to such a degree that it will not be improved merely by our assuming a pleasing attitude. Only a firm attitude on our part can prevent war with the United States. (quoted in Hosoya, 1976: 247–248)

Matsuoka's expectations of the effectiveness of coercive diplomacy failed to materialize in the wake of the pact, as American policy became even less accommodating.

FIVE

Stimson, Morgenthau, Hornbeck, and the Military

The U.S. army's viewpoint concerning strategies in Europe and in the Pacific and the assessments and recommendations formulated by the War Plans Division during 1940 and 1941 have already been mentioned. At this point, a more comprehensive examination of the army's approach to Japanese-American relations, juxtaposed with the views of the hard-liners, will help to distinguish between the policy advocated by the latter and the strategy recommended by the former.

The assessments made by U.S. army planners following the defeat of France in June 1940 remained basically unchanged until the Pearl Harbor attack. The army was convinced that in light of its limited resources, the United States should restrict itself to a single channel of action, namely, the defense of the Western Hemisphere, while striving to maintain peace in the Pacific. Both the army and the navy strongly believed that the defeat of France and the possible fall of Britain constituted greater threats to the security of the United States than any southward incursions by Japan. In Weigley's words (1973: 167), "By 1940 the likelihood of conflict with Japan had become much more than a matter of vague foreboding. By that time also, the rise of Hitler had confirmed the American army in its greater concern for European than for Asian interests. . . . From first to last, the leaders of the U.S. army hoped to avoid a Pacific war."

This belief formed the basis of the strategic plan, Rainbow 4, drafted in June 1940 by the War Plans Division. The plan stated that in the event of the elimination of British and French resistance and the termination of the war in Europe, followed by an "armed aggression in Asia," the United States was "to limit itself to defense of the entire Western Hemisphere, with American forces occupying British and French bases in the western Atlantic." Rainbow 4 called for a purely defensive position in the Pacific, and was approved in June by army chief of staff General George C. Marshall and chief of naval operations Admiral Harold R. Stark. Concurrently, General Marshall and Admiral Stark persuaded President Roosevelt that, if the French fleet passed to German control, the main body of American naval power would be transferred to the Atlantic. As Marshall (quoted in Weigley, 1973: 167; see also Morton, 1962: 75) observed: "A serious commitment in the Pacific is just what Germany would like us to undertake." Convinced that "every effort must be made to avoid [a Pacific] war," Marshall repeatedly insisted "on a clear restatement of military priorities that would place transatlantic interests first" (Wohlstetter, 1962: 230–231; Pogue, 1966: 194, 196; Weigley, 1973: 180).

Throughout the summer of 1940, several army planners continued to support a purely defensive position in the Pacific, although the Axis threat in Europe appeared to have abated somewhat. In late September, the danger in the Pacific again mounted as a result of the Japanese occupation of northern Indochina. Despite this menacing development, most military planners continued to share the belief that in light of the possibility of further "advances [by Japan] in the Far East [directed against] the Netherlands Indies or the Philippines . . . it would not be possible to oppose such moves by a major effort in the Pacific in view of the greater danger in the Atlantic. Operations in the Pacific should be held to the minimum" (Morton, 1962: 75; Weigley, 1973: 179–180).

One year later, during the months immediately preceding Pearl Harbor, this belief remained unchanged. Thus, on July 20, 1941, the director of the War Plans Division, Rear Admiral Richard K. Turner, observed in a memorandum to Admiral Stark:

> Speaking from the standpoint of self defense, the greatest danger to the United States in the future lies in the continued military success of Germany. . . . If Great Britain were to collapse, German military power might very well be directed against South America, and such moves would cause great difficulties for the

United States. So long as the United Kingdom continues to exist as a military and naval power, the problem of the United States as regards its security will not be very great. (U.S. Department of State, 1943: Vol. 2, Japan: 519)

Similarly, on November 3, 1941, the chief of the War Plans Division reasserted that "the principal objective in the Far East is to keep Japan out of the war." Two days later, Marshall and Stark restated to the president (quoted in Weigley, 1973: 185) that "Germany was more dangerous than Japan and must be defeated first, that the United States should avoid war with Japan if possible, and that if war with Japan came, it should be fought defensively until security across the Atlantic could be assured."

As the most appropriate means of accomplishing the strategic objective of avoiding a major commitment in the Pacific, several high-ranking army and navy officers recommended (Heinrichs, 1973: 219) a "cautious and restrained" policy toward Japan, to the extent that in November 1941 they fully supported the conclusion of a "truce" or modus vivendi agreement with the Japanese.

Indeed, both General Marshall and Admiral Stark (Pogue, 1966: 194) were painfully aware of "our state of unpreparedness," and convinced that "an unlimited Allied offensive against Japan would greatly weaken the combined effort against Germany, the most dangerous enemy." They were adamant in their opposition to "any word or action by the administration that might precipitate a crisis [in the Pacific]." Believing that "only if the United States yielded on several debating points could peace be saved," Chief of Staff Marshall in early November urged his government (quoted in Pogue, 1966: 196) "to make certain minor concessions which the Japanese could use in saving face. . . . These concessions [might be] a relaxation on oil restrictions or on similar trade restrictions." Also, after being shown on November 21, 1941, a preliminary version of the American modus vivendi plan (which was later abandoned), Admiral Stark and Brigadier-General Leonard T. Gerow, acting assistant chief of staff, agreed that "in general the document was satisfactory from a military standpoint." Gerow underlined his approval by sending in the following comment:

The adoption of its provisions would attain one of our present major objectives—the avoidance of war with Japan. Even a temporary peace in the Pacific would permit us to complete

defensive preparations in the Philippines and at the same time
insure continuance of material assistance to the British—both
of which are highly important. The foregoing should not be con-
strued as suggesting strict adherence to all the conditions outlined in the proposed agreement. War Plans Division wishes to
emphasize it is of grave importance to the success of our war
effort in Europe that we reach a *modus vivendi* with Japan.
(quoted in Wohlstetter, 1962: 237)

Thus, once a number of army officers had concluded that the threat
of a German victory over Britain would far outweigh any danger to the
United States resulting from Japanese expansion, and that the defense
of the Western Hemisphere was vital to the U.S. national interest, the
implications for the Pacific were clear. The army sought to pursue a defensive strategy which, coupled with a restrained policy toward Japan,
would enable the United States to concentrate its forces in the Atlantic
(Ben-Zvi, 1975: 236–237; see also Welles 1950: 97; Pogue, 1966: 194–196;
Weigley, 1973: 167–185).

As Wohlstetter (1962: 231) observes, during the period preceding the
outbreak of the Pacific War, "the War and Navy Departments in Washington expressed a clearly defined position. Admiral Stark and General
Marshall, solidly backed by their War Plans Divisions, sounded the plea
for more time, more men, more equipment. Their memos to the
President were all directed at soft-pedaling any State Department efforts
toward a 'firm stand' with Japan" (see also Perkins, 1957: 123; Pogue, 1966:
213).

This objective, together with its accompanying political implications,
was clearly expressed in November 1940 when Admiral Stark undertook
a comprehensive study of the military options open to the United States.
Known as the Plan Dog memorandum, the study (Memorandum for the
Secretary of the Navy Frank Knox, sent on November 12, 1940, in
President's Secretary's File [PSF], 1940: Navy Department; italics in original) argued strongly against major Far Eastern commitments involving the United States in an all-out military effort against Japan while
pointing out that such a course would siphon resources from the most
important theater, the Atlantic, and reduce aid to Britain. Stark's under-
lying premise was that "if Britain wins decisively against Germany—we
could win everywhere [, but] if she loses—the danger confronting us
would be very great; and, while we might not *lose everywhere*, we might,
possibly, not *win anywhere*." He asserted that "any strength that we might

send to the Far East would, by just so much, reduce the force of our blows against Germany and Italy." The Plan Dog memorandum clearly stated that "the continued existence of the British Empire, combined with building up a strong protection in our home areas [would] do most to ensure the status quo in the Western hemisphere, and to promote our principal national interests." In conclusion, the memorandum advised:

> Should we be forced into a war with Japan, we should—of course—because of the prospect of war in the Atlantic also, definitely plan to avoid operations in the Far East or the mid-Pacific that will prevent the Navy from promptly moving to the Atlantic forces fully adequate to safeguard our interests and policies in the event of a British collapse. We ought not now willingly engage in any war against Japan unless we are certain of aid from Great Britain and the Netherlands East Indies.

Following the military studies conducted during the first half of 1941, the war and navy secretaries approved, on June 2, a plan called Rainbow 5 which maintained that the major American military effort should be concentrated in the Atlantic, and (Morton, 1962: 90) once again relegated the Pacific theater to a secondary position. These basic strategic concepts were similarly prevalent throughout the course of the American-British staff meetings, known as the American-British Conversations, which began in Washington in January 1941. The American-British Conversations focused primarily on the "best methods by which the armed forces of the U.S. and the British Commonwealth [could] defeat Germany and the powers allied with her, should the United States be compelled to resort to war." During the meetings, the American staff representatives repeatedly indicated that if compelled to enter the war, the United States would "exert its principal military effort in the Atlantic area," would "limit operations in the Pacific and Far East [should Japan enter the war] to such a scope as not to interfere with concentration in the Atlantic," and would "hold to the defeat of the European Axis as the major goal of coalition strategy."

The British representatives did not always agree with this position, as the American desire to limit U.S. logistical commitments to Singapore contradicted the British view that "Singapore [was] the key to the defense of the British Commonwealth and its retention had thus to be assured." The American and British representatives failed to resolve these differences; the Americans clearly indicated that "no strengthening of

American forces in the Far East was even contemplated." In the words of General Sherman Miles (quoted in Leighton and Coakley, 1955: 52–54), "The British preoccupation with the Far East was diverting attention from their central problem, the security of the United Kingdom."

In light of these consecutive studies, memoranda, and strategic plans, it is clear that American military strategy for the Pacific reflected a continued determination to avoid war with Japan to the point of risking the loss of the Phillipines, Guam, and Wake Island. To what extent, then, was the policy which was urged so persistently by the hard-line group coordinated with the army's strategic conceptions and priorities? A first glance suggests that no discrepancy existed. After all, from May 1940 until the very eve of Pearl Harbor, the army consistently argued that the United States should do its utmost to avoid war with Japan and that the main military effort should be directed against Germany. The hard-liners also sought to deter Japan and thus avoid a military confrontation in the Pacific. Notwithstanding this superficial strategic similiarity between the two groups, however, they differed widely regarding the appropriate means for securing the objective of maintaining peace in the Pacific. The hard-liners advocated an aggressive policy of economic sanctions; the army called for restraint, conciliation, and even tactical concessions. Ultimately, Stimson and Morgenthau ignored the prospects of war inherent in the posture they so vigorously recommended. The hard-liners never seriously considered those views and military reports which in the most explicit and unequivocal terms warned that their course of action might, rather than leading to the desired outcome, instead provoke Japan to attack.

On those occasions when certain members of the hard-line group could not altogether ignore the army's reports and views advocating moderation, they tended to criticize the individuals expressing those views rather than to re-examine their own premises. Thus, on October 12, 1940, Stimson remarked in his diary:

> I have been reflecting on the subject [of what might be done by the U.S. Navy in the Pacific] of course for a long time and it is very evident that the heads of the Navy are rather cautious—unusually cautious men, and what seems to a good many of the Navy to be an important opportunity for bold, affirmative action is being strenuously opposed by the two men who are in highest position—Admiral Stark, the Chief of [Na-

val] Operations, and Admiral Richardson, the Commander of the Fleet. (1940: Vol 21, October 1–November 30).

On November 27, 1941, he similarly wrote:

> Stark is, as usual, a little bit timid and cautious when it comes to a real crisis, and there was a tendency . . . on his Part and [Brigadier-General Leonard T.] Gerow [acting assistant chief of staff] to seek for more time. I said that I was glad to have time but I didn't want it at any cost of humility on the part of the U.S. or of reopening the thing [the American-Japanese conversations] which would show a weakness on our part. (1941: Vol. 36, November 1–December 31)

The lack of coordination between the army's evaluations and recommendations and the policies supported by the hard-liners is evident in a memorandum prepared by Rear Admiral Turner on July 19, 1941. (The memorandum was approved by Admiral Stark, who on July 21 forwarded it to the president.) Formulated on the eve of the imposition of the de facto oil embargo upon Japan, the memorandum assessed the effects of further U.S. restrictions on exports to Japan and warned that "an embargo on exports [would create] an immediate severe psychological reaction in Japan against the United States." Turner concluded:

> It seems certain that, if Japan should then take military measures against the British and the Dutch, she would also include military action against the Philippines, which would immediately involve us in a Pacific war. . . .The embargo would probably result [, therefore,] in a fairly early attack by Japan on Malaya and the Netherlands East Indies, and possibly would involve the United States in an early war in the Pacific. (U.S. Congress, Pearl Harbor *Hearings*, 1946: Part 5, 2382–2384)

Thus, although in agreement with some of the army and navy evaluations of strategic needs and priorities, the hard-liners nevertheless failed to recognize the fundamental inconsistency between the policy they advocated and the army's strategic plans. They also failed to perceive the contradiction inherent in the simultaneous support of both military plans based on the need for restraint in the Pacific, and a posture advocating the imposition of comprehensive economic sanctions. In retrospect, the policy advocated by the hard-liners, instead of reducing the danger of war, only increased the likelihood of a Pacific conflagration.

In essence, the contradiction between the hard-liners and the army derived from differences in perspective. While the hard-liners were determined to oppose any nation which, in their view, participated in the worldwide effort to disrupt the global balance of power, the army's focus was on the impact that political and military developments (wherever they might occur) might have on the immediate security and vital interests of the United States (Neumann, 1957: 153). These incompatible perspectives created unbridgeable gaps between the policies promulgated by the two groups. A few examples will suffice to illustrate this dichotomy.

The hard-liners attempted, in close cooperation with Great Britain, to use economic sanctions to preserve (and later to restore) the balance of power in the Far East. This objective was an integral part of their overall policy line, and was designed to maintain the global balance of power and to prevent the collapse of England and the British Empire. However, several high-ranking army and navy officers, recognizing the tremendous burdens that a two-ocean war would impose on the United States, were determined to avoid any action that might lead to major military commitments in the Pacific—even when faced with the grim prospect of a renewed Japanese advance directed against the Dutch East Indies or the Philippines.

Similarly, when Japanese troops entered China, the hard-liners insisted on the immediate withdrawal of all Japanese forces from China as a prerequisite to any American-Japanese settlement. But the army desperately wanted to keep as much of the Japanese army as possible pinned down in China during the period following the German assault on Russia; it was aware that Japan's military involvement in China would reduce the possibility of the Japanese opening a front against Russia in Siberia. Thus the Japanese presence in China would help Russia in her struggle against Nazism—the objective that the army considered cardinal for American national security. Colonel Hayes A. Kroner, acting assistant chief of staff, stressed this argument in a memorandum to the chief of staff dated October 2, 1941:

The opportune moment [for launching Japan's attack upon Siberia] will be coincident with or immediately following a Russian collapse in Europe, or if and when the Russian forces become numerically inferior because of withdrawals from Siberia to reinforce the European armies. . . . From the foregoing it seems imperative, for the present at least, to keep as much of the Japanese Army as possible pinned down in China. In other words, we must cease at once our attempts to bring about the withdrawal of Japanese armed forces from China. . . . Our objective is the destruction of Nazism, and all-out aid to those powers actively engaged in resisting its aggressive drive. . . . Russia is, as a matter of expedience, an ally in this cause. We must . . . do what we can with what we have at our disposal to aid Russia in her struggle with Germany. Any action on our part, therefore, which would liberate Japanese forces for action against Russia's rear in Siberia would be foolhardy. (U.S. Congress, Pearl Harbor *Hearings*, 1946: Part 14, 1358)

Kroner's conclusion that insistence on the immediate evacuation of China "would be highly detrimental to our interests" was fully shared by the entire army intelligence service. As Schroeder observes,

The reports prepared by the Army Intelligence Service from July to December 1941 all display a single consistent point of view, along with a number of important insights. First was the belief that the European war remained uppermost and that the previous essentially defensive objectives pursued by the United States in the Far East should be maintained. Second was a recognition of the estrangement between Japan and Germany. Third was a belief that the Konoye government was really trying to extricate Japan from her difficulties without war. . . . *Fourth and most important was the conviction that it was unnecessary, and probably even harmful, for the United States to insist on an immediate evacuation of China.* (1958: 178–179, italics added)

Although the hard-liners regarded both Germany and Japan as the major initiators of the worldwide effort to disrupt the global balance of power, the army distinguished between the Atlantic and Pacific in terms of the danger to American national interests, and held that some of Japan's policies and military maneuvers were purely opportunistic. The army recognized that while Japanese policies did respond to developments in the European theater, they did not constitute part of a global scheme planned by the triumvirate of Germany, Italy, and Japan for the purpose of challenging the democracies and conquering the world.

Thus the army projected a picture of Japan's relations with her Axis allies that was much more dynamic, complex, and open to change than the one drawn by Morgenthau and Stimson, who perceived Japan as an inseparable part of the Axis coalition. Since it was capable of recognizing the various factors that strained Japanese-German relations, the army recommended certain broad policies which were designed to deepen those cleavages (Ben-Zvi, 1975: 238–239). On July 30, 1941, Brigadier-General Sherman Miles, in charge of army intelligence, sent a memorandum to the chief of staff:

> The time appears ripe for the judicious use of information which will have as its aim the dissolution of the Tripartite Pact. Any action on our part which will make Japan an even more reluctant Axis partner weakens our potential enemies, enhances our own prestige and authority, and materially and favorably affects our national defense. (U.S. Congress, Pearl Harbor *Hearings*, 1946: Part 14, 1356)

However, the United States did not translate this suggestion into action in 1941.

SIX

President Roosevelt
and Ambassador Grew:
The Pragmatic Approach

IMAGES AND POLICIES: A JUXTAPOSITION

A preliminary comparison of the respective belief systems of President Roosevelt and Ambassador Grew reveals markedly different images of Japan.

Although highly critical of some of Japan's policies, political factions, and leaders, Ambassador Grew had a very deep affection for that country, her culture and life style. As late as October 1942, when hatred and hostility overshadowed all other sentiments, Grew (quoted in Heinrichs, 1966: 364) continued to argue that "the average Japanese [was] a gentle, courteous, friendly [and] a beauty-loving person [and that] the very qualities that made Japan formidable as an enemy were qualities which, in other circumstances, could not only be respected but admired." Grew was always careful to distinguish between the various factions that operated on the Japanese political scene. Sensitive to the shifts and fluctuations in these groups' relative strength, he refrained from making sweeping generalizations about Japan and its leadership.

For example, in his cable from Tokyo, sent on June 3, 1940, Grew (quoted in Feis, 1950: 62) reported "great differences of opinion as regards the nature of a settlement with China and the means of bringing it about." According to his analysis, "one influential group was advocating an agreement with the Soviet Union to divide China; and some of its members were urging as well the seizure of the Indies before the final German victory. Another group was basing its program upon close alliance with Germany against Britain." But, Grew further observed, "there were still steadfast advocates of the view that Japan should seek to settle the war in China by cooperation with the democracies, and refrain from the use of force anywhere else."

Grew was profoundly impressed by various aspects of Japanese culture (to which he was continuously exposed), and his background images of Japan were correspondingly sympathetic. He was fully committed to these perceptions, and consistently believed that normal and peaceful relations between the United States and Japan could be maintained "provided *both* refrained from mutual recriminations and conducted their day-to-day affairs in a spirit of pragmatism and moderation." Grew was also contemptuous of the "generally accepted theory" that Japan "has always been the big bully and China the downtrodden innocent." He conceived of an Asia in which "the legitimate interests of the Japanese empire could be reconciled with those of China, America, and the British Empire without necessitating any armed conflict" (Iriye, 1973: 126).

On the other hand, Roosevelt, during the first thirty-one years of his political life, had maintained a stereotyped vision of Japan, according to which the Japanese were the "Prussians of the East, and just as drunk with their dreams of domination." Pelz (1974: 75) notes that: "In Roosevelt's eyes . . . Japan was an unstable, aggressive, and dangerous country with long-range plans to establish a vast empire and with no compunctions against defying the desire of the world for peace and disarmament."

Roosevelt's initial image of Japan was formed as an antithesis of his romantic and idealistic image of China. During his childhood, he had been exposed to "stories of the dealings [which] members of his family had had with various Chinese dignitaries and merchants in the earlier decades of the nineteenth century" (Welles, 1950: 68). His grandfather, Warren Delano, had served in China "as the agent of the State Department" during the Civil War, and Roosevelt inherited from his mother's side of the family a "deep feeling of friendship for China" (Hofstadter, 1957: 339). This deep-rooted sympathy toward China, which Roosevelt developed during the early phases of his political socialization and upbringing, was later readily recognized by him on various occasions. For example, writing on September 28, 1941, to Allan Forbes, president of the State Street Trust Company in Boston, Roosevelt reminisced (President's

Personal File [PPF], 1941: Box 490) that his mother, Sara Delano, "always thought and talked so much of those early days in China—and up to the last she was greatly interested in the great struggle which the Chinese [were] making to retain their independence." This romantic perception of China a priori dictated animosity toward Japan—the power which posed a threat to China's territorial integrity.

A revealing illustration of this dichotomous vision of the Far East can be found in a letter which Roosevelt sent on December 16, 1937, to Rhoda Hinkley, an acquaintance from Dutchess County, in which he asserted:

> I happen to know a very nice Chinese family which lives quite far in the interior. For years they have said that China wanted peace at any price and that they felt no possible harm could come to them back from the seacoast. The other day most of the family was wiped out by some Japanese bombing planes which wrecked their community and killed one thousand people. I got a message from one of the survivors which read: "We are no longer for peace at any price." (PPF, Box 1990)

Further reinforced by a departmental perspective (the navy depicted Japan as a highly dangerous adversary), this background image suffused Roosevelt's thinking during the period in which he served as assistant secretary of the navy in President Wilson's cabinet. According to Sumner Welles (1950: 68), Roosevelt "had then become imbued with the Navy's conviction that Japan was America's number-one antagonist." In 1913, Roosevelt (quoted in Range, 1959: 80) repeatedly expressed the view that Japan was "the most powerful potential enemy of the U.S. and that the Navy should be kept prepared for trouble with her." Twenty years later, in January 1933, he accused Japan of imperialistic ambitions "that were likely in the coming decade to cause the world much trouble." Similarly, in a letter to the Reverend Malcolm E. Peabody[1] dated August 19, 1933, (PPF, 1933: Box 732), President Roosevelt again voiced his apprehension about Japanese naval strength, remarking that "the whole scheme of things in Tokyo [did] not make for an assurance of non-aggression in the future." "As a matter of fact," he continued, "our [naval] building program . . . will barely suffice to keep us almost up to the ship strength of the Japanese Navy and still, of course, far below the British Navy. I am not concerned about the latter but I am about the first."

Furthermore, on May 17, 1934, in the course of a meeting between President Roosevelt and Henry Stimson (described in Stimson's *Diary*, 1934: Vol. 27, entry of May 17), the president quite vividly recalled the details of a conversation with a Japanese friend which had been held thirty-two year earlier, while Roosevelt was a sophomore in college. According to Stimson's account, Roosevelt's Japanese acquaintance had revealed to him the existence of a plan, secretly formulated in 1899, for the establishment of a "Japanese dynasty," which he called "the hundred years plan." The plan consisted of ten consecutive steps, culminating (in 1999) in the "establishment of Japanese[2] . . . over all of the yellow races, including the Malays [which would enable Japan] to have a definite point of threat against Europe." Japan would also secure control over Manchuria and establish a protectorate over northern China (step 1); "absorb Korea" (step 2); "conduct a defensive war against Russia" (step 3); "acquire all the islands of the Pacific including Hawaii" (step 8); and eventually occupy Australia and New Zealand (step 9).

It is amazing that the president was capable of remembering, in such detailed form, a plan related to him in 1902. Even more striking is the fact that in 1934 he apparently re-examined the scheme in all seriousness, concluding that, in light of such developments as Japan's expansion to Manchuria, there might be some grain of truth in it. Indeed, it is unlikely that Roosevelt would have so vividly remembered such an episode unless he believed in some of the plan's basic premises. Eleanor Roosevelt supports this view, writing in her memoirs:

> My husband had long suspected that these Japanese dreams of grandeur and domination existed. I remember his concern about Guam and the other islands of the Pacific as far back as when he was assistant secretary of the Navy. . . . His suspicion of Japan was based on his own ideas of what made the Pacific safe for us, and in all the war games in the Pacific, Japan was always the enemy. (1949: 235)

As a means of combating this frightening vision of the growing Japanese menace, the president contemplated, in the wake of the *Panay* incident of December 1937, a plan to blockade Japan "on a line from the Aleutians through Hawaii to Guam," and that "the British could take over the patrol from Guam to Singapore" (Pelz, 1974: 76). As Secretary Ickes noted in his diary upon hearing Roosevelt's idea articulated on December 18, 1937 (Ickes, Vol. 2, 1953: 274; Pelz, 1974: 76), "This would be a comparatively simple task which the Navy could take care of without having to send a great fleet. Blocked thus, the President thinks that Japan could be brought to her knees within a year."

Finally, the evidence from 1939 on indicates that Roosevelt identified Japan with Nazi Germany, viewing them as "two forces of evil" which should be "purged of the evil in them" through "a major surgical operation on their body politics" (Range, 1959: 80; Dallek, 1979: 237).

Thus, separated from each other by virtue of fundamentally different background images and experiences, Grew and Roosevelt formed incompatible, dichotomous perceptions of Japan. Nevertheless, Roosevelt did not allow his preliminary visions of Japan to automatically dictate his actual behavior during the period preceding the Pearl Harbor attack. Although his operational code reflected unbounded animosity and suspicion toward the Japanese, this was mitigated by the predilections that constituted the instrumental strata of his belief system (George, 1969: passim). Essentially a pragmatist "who favored an approach that would take power realities into account" (George, 1980: 239), he was bound to deviate occasionally from the moralistic and universalistic Wilsonian tradition to which he adhered in theory (Sherwood, 1948: 227, 266; Osgood, 1953: 410–411; Greer, 1958: 10, 88; Schlesinger, 1967: 27; George, 1980: 239). In the words of Osgood,

> In some ways President Roosevelt was a spiritual descendant of Woodrow Wilson. There can be no doubt that he was deeply impressed with America's moral responsibility for promoting peace, democracy, and a better way of living throughout the world. . . . At the same time, there was a streak of pragmatism in Roosevelt that saved him from Wilson's extravagant moral expectations. There was a subtlety of nature and a temporizing quality which allowed him to accept the half-loaf. Moreover, he was keenly aware of the practical failure of Wilson's lofty objectives and determined to avoid a repetition of his mistakes. (1953: 410–411)

Roosevelt himself readily acknowledged his general propensity to improvise rather than to adhere rigidly to abstract formulas. On December 9, 1940, in a personal letter to Malcolm E. Peabody, the president (PPF, 1940: Box 732) noted, "Actually, I am not as worried as you are because when some practical situation arises, good sense seems to prevail in the long run." Similarly, in a letter to Ambassador Grew dated January

21, 1941, Roosevelt admitted (President's Secretary's File [PSF], 1941: No. 46: Japan-Diplomatic Correspondence, January-September), "In conclusion, I must emphasize that, our problem being one of defense, we cannot lay down hard and fast plans. As each new development occurs, we must, in the light of circumstances then existing, decide when and where and how we can most effectively marshal and make use of our resources."

Likewise, during one of his press conferences, the president drew a comparison between his methods as a statesman and the strategies used by the quarterback in a football game. This was done in an attempt to illustrate his tendency to improvise and proceed pragmatically, rather than to take a rigid approach. Maintaining that, like the quarterback, he knew "what the next play [would] be," Roosevelt pointed out (quoted in Hofstadter, 1957: 237) that beyond the next play, however, neither he nor the quarterback could "predict or plan too rigidly because future plays [would] depend on how the next one [worked]."

This recognition of practical considerations was labeled a "happy-go-lucky opportunism" by Herbert Feis, who in 1937 was an official in the Treasury Department (conversation between Feis and Stimson, in Stimson's *Diary*, 1937: Vol. 28). It was clearly evident in Roosevelt's actual behavior toward Japan during 1940 and 1941. As Burns points out, the cluster of global issues confronting the United States during the period preceding Pearl Harbor was not perceived by the president in a "systemic, categorized frame." Instead,

> he still preferred to deal with situations piecemeal, plucking the Army's problem out of the tangle of events, turning it over, seeing its involvement in wider issues but not trying to deal with them as a whole. He was not seeking to be a grand strategist. . . . If Roosevelt was not making strategy, he was still recognizing priorities—especially the Atlantic over the Pacific. He felt that his policy of babying the Japanese along, of keeping them off balance, after two years was holding off a showdown in the Pacific. (1970: 107)

Indeed, unlike the hard-liners, whose background images had short-term direct behavioral ramifications in determining their policy preferences in 1940 and 1941, President Roosevelt tended to react increasingly to the immediate, specific crisis situations and less to his basic images, which subsided into the background (see, in this connection, George, 1969: 200; Stein and Brecher 1976: 35–37; Lockhart, 1977: 384; Snyder and Diesing, 1977: 329–332; Hermann, 1978: 57). Preoccupied with the European war (which was perceived by him as *the* major threat to American security) and uncertain as to Japan's immediate intentions in 1941, Roosevelt was thus prepared to abandon the moral mission of performing a "major surgical operation on Japan's body politic" for the sake of reaching a modus vivendi agreement in the Pacific. This would enable the United States, he surmised, to transfer its entire Pacific fleet to the Atlantic and thus concentrate on the front he regarded as the more crucial one. In this respect he differed markedly from the hard-liners, who "knew" from the outset of the crisis what Japan's objectives were, and complained from time to time about the president's vacillation and lack of decisiveness in the face of the approaching danger. As Wohlstetter (1962: 233) points out (regarding Roosevelt's state of mind in November 1941), "Again, as in the debate on whether to continue basing the fleet at Pearl Harbor, the President did not know which way to move." Fearing, like Grew, that the uncompromising posture vehemently recommended by the hard-liners might provoke Japan rather than deter her, the president—"whose personal hatred of war was deep and genuine" (Divine, 1969: 43)—was willing to set aside ideological considerations for the sake of neutralizing the threat of an immediate war in the Pacific.

During the period preceding the outbreak of the Pacific War, this willingness on Roosevelt's part to decouple his pre-existing image of Japan's long-term objectives from his immediate perceptions of some of her specific actions was manifested on numerous occasions. For example, in June 1940, the secretary of the Treasury requested that responsibility for the export of strategic materials be delegated to the Treasury Department, hoping that this would enable him to impose a de facto embargo on oil and steel shipments to Japan. Morgenthau's request was turned down by the president, causing Morgenthau to note disappointedly in his diary entry of July 26, 1940 (quoted in Blum, 1970: 391) that Roosevelt wanted "to do it in his own way and to keep the authority under himself." As Dallek notes,

> Believing that strong measures would provoke an unwanted Pacific crisis and that appeasement would encourage further Japanese demands, [Roosevelt and Hull] continued to urge a middle ground. . . . A conflict with Japan would not only reduce Anglo-American power to defeat Berlin, it would also jeopardize the President's political future. Having just been nominated for a third term on a platform of no participation in foreign wars

unless attacked, Roosevelt felt constrained to avoid provocative
steps. (1979: 239)

Similarly, in October 1940 Roosevelt strongly objected to Morgenthau's pleas for a strong policy against Japan, reminding him
(quoted in Langer and Gleason, 1953: 35) that the president and the
secretary of state alone were "handling foreign affairs." The subject of
partial embargoes against Japan came up again in a meeting with Cordell Hull, Sumner Welles, and Breckenridge Long on October 10, 1940,
and "the President's position was that we were not to shut off oil from
Japan . . . and thereby force her into a military expedition against the
Dutch East Indies but we were to withhold from Japan only such things
as we vitally needed ourselves, such as high test gas" (quoted in Anderson, 1975: 143).

One month later, on November 13, 1940, Roosevelt again expressed his
opposition to harsh economic measures against Japan. Responding to
an appeal from his wife that American policy be changed, he wrote:

> The real answer you cannot use is that if we forbid oil shipments
> to Japan, Japan will increase her purchases of Mexican oil and,
> furthermore, may be driven by actual necessity to a descent on
> the Dutch East Indies. At this writing, we all regard such action
> on our part as an encouragement to the spread of war in the Far
> East. (quoted in E. Roosevelt, 1950: Vol. 2, 1173)

Furthermore, when a new crisis arose over reports of a Japanese offensive against northern Indochina, "circumstances dictated that
Roosevelt not challenge Japan." As Dallek (1979: 273–274) observes,
"Though he considered giving a strong response, the battle of the
Atlantic and the Lend-Lease debate constrained him. . . . Instead of
strong measures, Roosevelt relied on 'moral steps' of doubtful consequence."

Similarly, during June and July 1941, President Roosevelt repeatedly
urged moderation, fearing that drastic economic sanctions "might be a
prelude to war." Thus, on June 18, he opposed Secretary Ickes's attempt,
following his appointment as petroleum coordinator for national defense, to use his newly acquired administrative powers to impose a de
facto embargo on oil shipments to Japan. He explained to Ickes:

The Japanese are having a real drag-down and knock-out fight among themselves . . . trying to decide which way they are going to jump—attack Russia, attack the South Seas (thus throwing in their lot definitely with Germany), or whether they will sit on the fence and be more friendly with us. No one knows what the decision will be but . . . it is terribly important for the control of the Atlantic for us to help keep peace in the Pacific. I simply have not got enough to go round—and every little episode in the Pacific means fewer ships in the Atlantic. (*The Morgenthau Diary*, 1941: Book 410, June 18–19)

Finally, on several occasions during the Atlantic Conference of August 1941, the president refused to give Churchill "an assurance that [he] would go to Congress for authority to give armed support" if Japan attacked British or Dutch possessions, reiterating his conviction that "every effort should be made to prevent the outbreak of war with Japan." The premise behind Roosevelt's continual advocacy of moderation, lest Japan be pushed to retaliate, was most clearly and comprehensively expressed during a meeting that he held on July 24, 1941, with the Volunteer Participation Committee of the Office of Civilian Defense. Indeed, so uninhibited was the president in his informal and extemporaneous remarks that it is instructive to quote him at some length:

Here on the east coast, you have been reading that the Secretary of the Interior [Ickes], as Oil Administrator, is faced with the problem of not having enough gasoline to go around in the east coast, and how he is asking everybody to curtail their consumption of gasoline. All right. Now, I am—I might be called an American citizen living in Hyde Park, New York, and I say: "That's a funny thing. Why am I asked to curtail my consumption of gasoline when I read in the papers that thousands of tons of gasoline are going out from Los Angeles—west coast—to Japan; and we are helping Japan in what looks like an act of aggression?" All right. Now the answer is a very simple one. There is a world war going on, and has been for some time—nearly two years. One of our efforts, from the very beginning, was to prevent the spread of that world war in certain areas where it hadn't started. One of those areas is a place called the Pacific Ocean—one of the largest areas of the earth. There happened to be a place in the South Pacific where we had to get a

lot of things—rubber, tin, and so forth and so on—down in the
Dutch Indies, the Straits Settlements, and Indo-China. And we
had to help get the Australian surplus of meat and wheat and
corn for England.

It was very essential from our own selfish point of view of
defense to prevent war from starting in the South Pacific. . . .
All right. And here is a nation called Japan. . . . Now, if we
[had] to cut the oil off, they probably would have gone down to
the Dutch East Indies a year ago, and you would have had a war.
Therefore, there was, you might call, a method in letting this oil
to Japan, with the hope—and it has worked for two years—of
keeping war out of the South Pacific for our own good, for the
good of the defense of Great Britain, and the freedom of the seas.
(Rosenman, 1950: Vol. 1, 279–280)

Indeed, demonstrating "an apparent disdain for fixed principles"
(Divine, 1969: 5), the president preferred a restrained course of action in
the Pacific, in the hope that such a flexible posture could avert war and
thus enable the United States to concentrate its attention and resources
in the central, most crucial theater—the Atlantic. Furthermore, while
Stimson and Morgenthau based their policy recommendations on certain "lessons from the past," which they mechanically and indiscrim-
inately applied to the context of American-Japanese relations, President
Roosevelt believed that such analogies were neither appropriate nor
valuable. This skepticism was clearly expressed during a press conference held on June 5, 1940:

And I do not think frankly, [that] it is an awful lot of use to talk
about the past. . . . I do not think you get a long distance forward in trying to pass judgment in a very critical time today on
episodes that are closed episodes. I really do not think you get
very far. It is an awful thing to say, but what good does it do?
Where do you stop? Why not go back to the Franco-Prussian
war and ask questions about that? It is not so long ago—seventy
years ago—why not go back twenty years, thirty years, forty
years? I am not, frankly, interested in past history because
current events that are beginning to form history are of much,
much greater importance than trying to go back and rehash
things in the past. (Roosevelt, 1933–1945, *Press Conferences*, 1940:
Vol. 1, January 1–June 30, Box 235)

A juxtaposition of the premises upon which President Roosevelt based his *preferred* Far Eastern strategy during 1940 and 1941 and those adhered to by Ambassador Grew indicates that while the two differed in their basic perception of Japan, they nevertheless supported, on the eve of the Pacific War, an essentially identical posture—at least in principle (Grew, 1952: 1228–1229; Toland, 1970: 106–107). Thus, just as Roosevelt was highly skeptical of the policy of "getting tough" with Japan, Grew repeatedly expressed concern that "an embargo would set relations on the downward slope of retaliation and counter-retaliation leading toward war." "Mr. Stimson and his satellites," Grew sarcastically remarked on one occasion (quoted in Heinrichs, 1966: 342, and Iriye, 1973: 122–123), "dangerously underestimated the attendant risk of war."[3]

In many of the telegrams he sent to Washington throughout 1938–1941, Grew repeatedly warned against assuming that continued economic pressure would force Japan to yield and withdraw. In his cable of November 3, 1941 (PSF, Box 30), for example, he emphasized that "Japanese sanity could not be measured by our standards of logic," and that consequently, Japan's capacity "to rush headlong into a suicidal conflict with the United States" should not be underestimated. Should all efforts to reach a political settlement fail, he warned cryptically in this message, "the pendulum in Japan will in all probability swing once more to its former [extremist] position." And while, as the ambassador asserted in his cable of December 14, 1940 (PSF, 1940: Box 59; Japan: January-September), economic obstacles "such as may arise from American embargoes, will seriously handicap Japan in the long run," they would tend—in the short run—"to push the Japanese onward in a forlorn hope of making themselves economically self-sufficient. . . . A progressively firm policy on our part [he therefore concluded] will entail inevitable risks—especially risks of sudden uncalculated strokes."

As early as April 1938, when Hornbeck asked Grew for "the probable Japanese response to definite steps in the field of positive pressure by the United States," the ambassador predicted that the Japanese government would regard any form of sanction as a hostile act. He observed (quoted in Pratt, 1964: 494–495) that in such an eventuality the Japanese government would most probably "be replaced by an out-and-out military dictatorship," while the Japanese people would become strongly anti-American and generally xenophobic.

One and a half years later, in his diary entry of November 1939 which he enclosed in his letter to the president of December 21, 1939 (POF, Box 204, Joseph C. Grew, 1933–1944), Grew similarly cautioned that

"estimates [regarding the prospects of:] defeating Japan by economic
sanctions . . . based on statistics alone may well mislead," since the statis-
ticians "generally fail to include psychological factors in their estimates," including the fact that "Japan is a nation of hardy warriors, still
inculcated with the samurai do-or-die spirit which has by tradition and
inheritance become ingrained in the race." On the very eve of Pearl
Harbor, he again predicted—in his dispatch of November 30, 1941—that
a continued irreconcilable posture toward Japan would lead to an "all-
out, do or die attempt, actually risking *hara-kiri*, to make Japan impervi-
ous to economic embargoes abroad."

> If the fiber and temper of the Japanese people are kept in mind,
> the view that war probably would be averted . . . by progres-
> sively imposing drastic economic pressures is an uncertain and
> dangerous hypothesis upon which to base considered U.S. policy
> and measures. War would not be averted by such a course . . . in
> the opinion of the Embassy. . . . It would be shortsighted for
> American policy to be based upon the belief that Japanese
> preparations are no more than saber rattling. . . . Action by
> Japan which might render unavoidable an armed conflict with
> the U.S. may come with dangerous and drastic suddenness. (PSF,
> Box 30)

In order to avert such a conflagration, Grew urged "constructive tran-
sigence" (Grew's diary entry of November 1939, enclosed in his letter to
the President of December 21, 1939 [POF, Box 204, Joseph C. Grew,
1933–1944]), that is, the pursuit of a pragmatic, flexible policy, respon-
sive to changing circumstances in Japan and sensitive to shifts in the
Japanese attitude toward the United States, as opposed to a doctrinaire
insistence on the immediate implementation of all American principles
(Emmerson, 1978: 84). In light of Premier Konoye's moderation and his
willingness, in the summer of 1941, to disregard the Tripartite Pact de
facto (which Grew was quick to recognize), Grew was prepared to sacrifice certain long-term American objectives in order to promote "American national objectives, policies, and needs" (Schroeder, 1958: 209–211).

Convinced that the Japanese political scene was characterized by
divergence and complexity, Grew advocated a strategy of accommodation which sought to strengthen the bargaining position of the
moderate elements in the Japanese government vis-à-vis the more mili-

tant and intransigent factions. As he wrote the president on September 22, 1941:

> As you know from my telegrams, I am in close touch with Prince Konoye who, in the face of bitter antagonism from extremist and pro-Axis elements in the country, is courageously working for an improvement in Japan's relations with the United States. Whatever the incentive that has led to [Konoye's] present efforts, I am convinced that he now means business and will go as far as is possible, without incurring open rebellion in Japan, to reach a reasonable understanding with us. It seems to me highly unlikely that this chance [of a settlement] will come again or that any Japanese statesman other than Prince Konoye could succeed in controlling the military extremists in carrying through a policy which they, in their ignorance of international affairs and economic laws, resent and oppose. . . . I therefore most earnestly hope that we can come to terms, even if we must take on trust, at least to some degree, the continued good faith . . . of the present Government. (PSF, 1941: Box 59, Japan: January–September)

Grew's policy toward Japan was thus derived from the belief that there was nothing immutable in the Japanese attitude toward the United States (or toward her Axis partners) and that Japan's foreign policy and diplomacy were essentially susceptible to world developments and events. He was convinced that a considerable amount of common interest did exist in the relations between the United States and Japan, and was therefore predisposed to advocate an accommodative posture, fearing that too much reliance on uncompromising firmness might be misinterpreted by the Japanese as a design for aggression, and would thus elicit retaliatory behavior. Grew perceived the Japanese opponent as a differentiated unit, whose enmity was transient and remediable. He therefore differed sharply from Stimson, Morgenthau, and Hornbeck, whose intransigent behavior toward Japan was predicated upon their belief that the Pacific crisis was merely one element within a larger, worldwide context. Translated into specific terms, Grew's pragmatism and moderation bore a striking resemblance to the president's immediate images. And these, decoupled from Roosevelt's basic perceptions, determined his preferences and initial policy recommendations (albeit not the policy ultimately pursued) during the Far Eastern crisis of 1940 and 1941.

And indeed, both the president and the ambassador were aware that the continuation of a policy of severe economic sanctions might lead to a war in the Pacific for which the United States was unprepared. Thus, despite incompatible background images, they both supported a modus vivendi agreement in the hope that it would introduce a measure of stability into the fragile and tense framework of American-Japanese relations. While they did not expect the proposed agreement to settle all the controversial issues, Roosevelt and Grew were hopeful that it would settle the most pressing ones, thus reducing the danger of war without necessarily sacrificing all the American principles and long-term objectives.

An examination of Roosevelt's original modus vivendi proposal and Grew's numerous cables throughout 1941 indicates that both aimed at a limited and temporary agreement with Japan which would create a more conciliatory and dispassionate atmosphere, thereby strengthening the moderate faction within the Japanese leadership. Thus in his original modus vivendi proposal, the president was willing to leave in abeyance the complicated issue of China while settling other urgent questions, such as Japan's southward military advance. Suggesting a similar approach, Grew (PSF, 1941: Box 59, Japan: January-September) maintained, in a typical message dated September 4, 1941, that an effort should be made to "ease the immediate issues, such as Japan's southward advance," as a means for "improving the atmosphere," thus paving the way for a settlement of the Chinese question. Essentially, both Roosevelt and Grew clearly distinguished between long-range goals and certain "core interests" in U.S. foreign policy; they were acutely aware of the folly of demanding the immediate realization of both categories (Osgood, 1953: 358; Heinrichs, 1966: 344). As Grew observed,

> Our long-range objectives are based on our belief in the wisdom and efficacy of the universal adoption and maintenance of certain fundamental principles in the conduct of international affairs. . . . Obviously the attainment of these [long-range objectives] was of its nature not an immediate possibility and was predicated upon the existence in the world of certain conditions which could not be obtained until the termination of the European war. . . . The immediate objectives of our foreign policy, on the other hand, vary of necessity in accordance with shifting

conditions and may be defined as the protection and maintenance of those vital national interests without whose preservation there could be no hope of attaining our [long-range] goals.
(1952: 1255)

It is clear, therefore, that throughout the period 1940–1941, the dominant factor in the thinking of both Roosevelt and Grew was a set of
pragmatic considerations derived from a narrowly defined perception of
American national interests. While they also considered other
concepts—such as "realistic globalism" based upon the notion of the balance of power, and "idealistic cosmopolitanism" predicated on international law—they were *essentially* motivated, in formulating their specific
policy recommendations toward Japan, by a cluster of pragmatic-
nationalistic premises (Ben-Zvi, 1975: 236).

However, notwithstanding his predilection for an accommodative
strategy, the president was severely constrained in his efforts to implement his preferred course of action in the Pacific. His preoccupation
with many other issues, such as developments in the European war,
prevented him from systematically and forcefully directing U.S. policy
toward Japan. In addition, the president was subjected to pressures to
harden American policy toward Japan, exerted not only by several
members of the cabinet but also by a number of prominent public figures, congressmen, party leaders, pressure groups (such as the Price
Committee), and public opinion leaders, as well as several members of
his own family. Indeed, moralistic outrage at Japanese military aggression, legalistic opposition to Japanese violation of the Nine Power Pact
and the Pact of Paris, internationalist desire to guard peace and security
through measures short of war, and special interests of specific economic groups "all encouraged the Roosevelt administration. . . . to favor
various economic restrictions against Japan" (Cole, 1973: 317–318).

As Cole further observes in analyzing the prevailing congressional
mood during the period preceding Pearl Harbor,

Congressmen and party leaders did not want war with Japan,
but that possibility disturbed them less than involvement in Europe. The administration's actions short of war against Japan
won widespread approval from legislators in both parties.
Indeed, many were impatient with the administration for its
failure to block the flow of goods to Japan sooner and more
completely. (1973: 303–304)

Not only was the president provided (by Stimson, Morgenthau, and Ickes) with carefully selected opinions and interpretations (including excerpts from newspaper editorials) which advocated coercive diplomacy in the Pacific, but he was occasionally subjected to more direct forms of pressure. In an attempt to persuade him to harden American policy toward Japan, some of the letters and petitions which were sent to Roosevelt by various public figures (such as the governor of Oregon, Charles A. Sprague, and the governor of California, Culbert L. Olson) and organizations (such as the Price Committee and the Washington Committee for Non-Participation in Japanese Aggression) were exceedingly blunt in style and content. (For evidence regarding the intensive lobbying activities of Roger S. Greene, chairman of the Price Committee, see PPF, Box 5826.) For example, in an urgent petition to the president drafted by the Washington Committee for Non-Participation in Japanese Aggression on July 10, 1940, the following paragraphs were included:

16. Do you [the president] know that so-called "rapprochement or appeasement policies" of the U.S. toward Japan are as futile as were the Chamberlain policies of appeasing Hitler?
17. Do you know that if such "appeasement" policies are pursued, that within a year the U.S. may be obliged to fight unaided, with our one-ocean navy, enemy powers on both our Atlantic and Pacific coasts? (POF, 1940: Japan)

Another form of consistent, albeit more subtle, pressure was institutionalized by Stimson in December 1940 when he established the nucleus of an economic warfare staff as a "study group" in the Army Industrial College. By early May 1941, this group "had produced and circulated no less than eighteen contingency plans on how to cripple Japan economically, with only passing reference to whether such a policy shoud be adopted" (Anderson, 1975: 269).

Toward the end of 1941, the multiplicity of pressures directed at Roosevelt proved to be effective as he gradually abandoned his preferred accommodative position. Thus, despite the president's awareness of the possible repercussions of economic sanctions, American policy was characterized by increasing inflexibility. True, the constraints exerted on Roosevelt did not always persuade him to abandon altogether his original skepticism regarding the efficacy of applying economic sanctions against Japan. However, as the president was sensitive to the mood of the nation (which was clearly hostile to Japan) and was simultaneously preoccupied with the course of the European war, he did not insist that all his initial recommendations be carried out to the letter. He was therefore predisposed to deviate from some of his original policy recommendations, and to seek compromise formulas that would satisfy public opinion and minimize internal divisions.

Some of the decisions made by the president were ambiguous, leaving ample room for differing interpretations by the various departments and agencies responsible for their implementation, primarily the Treasury Department. For example, fearing that "to cut off oil altogether at this time would probably precipitate an outbreak of war in the Pacific" (quoted in Anderson, 1975: 175), Roosevelt did not seek to impose upon Japan a *complete* oil embargo in the wake of the Japanese occupation of southern Indochina in late July 1941. Yet the fact that his instructions lacked precision (and that he left Washington on August 3 for secret talks with Churchill at Argentia, Newfoundland) enabled the Treasury Department, the Interdepartmental Foreign Funds Control Committee, and the Economic Defense Board to use their administrative power and licensing prerogatives to effectively block virtually all shipments of oil to Japan as of August 1, 1941. As Anderson observes,

> In retrospect, the chief product of Japan's occupation of southern Indochina was not an oil embargo, but an unguided bureaucracy biased at the working level against liberality toward Japan. Although by mid-September this maze has congealed into a *de facto* embargo, it should be clear from the above account that this end was not Roosevelt's original intent. The initial termination of shipments from both the United States and the Indies was purely the result of a bureaucratic tangle as various agencies, governments, and companies attempted to discern the real intent of American policy and adjust their own actions accordingly. . . . All those involved in oil shipments felt that American attitudes were becoming increasingly tough minded, and from August no one was inclined to unsnarl the tangle and to be the first to release a shipment. . . . Bureaucratic momentum carried the day. (1975: 178–179)

Ultimately, then, President Roosevelt's inability to systematically and forcefully direct American policy toward Japan (and his absence from the scene at a most crucial junction in American-Japanese relations), combined with Grew's lack of influence in the decision-making process, resulted in the development of a policy which—although in accordance with Roosevelt's preliminary background images—did not reflect his immediate perceptions and assessments of the unfolding crisis in the Pacific in 1940 and 1941. In George's terminology (1980: 248–250), the president, faced with a plethora of domestic pressures and constraints, and hence with the expected difficulty of achieving "adequate legitimation" for a more accommodative posture in the Pacific, shied away from trying to educate public opinion to support his preferred strategy of realistic-pragmatism. Unwilling to alienate the pro-internationalist forces whose support was essential in the struggle to contain Hitler in Europe, he was therefore compelled, on the eve of war, to set aside his idea of an American-Japanese modus vivendi.

AN APPRAISAL

In evaluating the policies advocated by President Roosevelt and Ambassador Grew, it is essential to analyze the decision-making process within the Roosevelt administration, particularly during the second half of 1941.

In effect, Grew did not contribute to this process. The gap between his on-the-scene perceptions and those of the Washington policy elite was the principal cause of his lack of substantial involvement in the policy-making process. As his October 1939 public attack on Japan's continued invasion of China and his September 1940 "green light" message clearly illustrate, Grew did not uncritically accept the Japanese point of view. He was "absolutely opposed" to such policies as "Japan's southern advance" and her actions in China (Osgood, 1953: 357). And at the opposite end of the scale, several of his reports during the summer of 1941 gave an overoptimistic evaluation of Konoye's ability both to carry out a peace program and to persuade the army to evacuate China. These reports are open to criticism on the ground that the ambassador underestimated several factors of which he was aware, such as the army's considerable influence in formulating Japan's policy toward China. Serious as these shortcomings were, however, they by no means justify the fact that Grew's observations and evaluations were completely ignored.

Although Grew was an experienced diplomat, possessing a broad complex of information about Japan's internal political structure, culture, and patterns of behavior, he was totally deprived of any influence in the formation of U.S. Policy toward Japan (Toland, 1970: 107).

It has been argued that Grew's recommendations should not have been accepted by the Roosevelt administration because, in his advocacy of a settlement with Japan at the expense of China, he ignored the "vital principles of the U.S. and its moral task in the world." However, an examination of Grew's recommendations suggests that he never advocated an entirely Machiavellian policy. Instead, he supported a strategy that reflected a particular moral preference for maintaining peace in the Pacific. Convinced that Hull erred in his belief that America's prime moral duty was to adhere to abstract principles regardless of the consequences, Grew still recognized that stability in the Pacific was both a moral and a practical goal, the achievement of which did not require the United States to abandon altogether its support for China's sovereignty (Schroeder, 1958: 208–216; Iriye, 1973: 125).

Not only was Grew completely unsuccessful in attempting to influence his government's policies but during the latter half of 1941, in the aftermath of Hull's about-face, his influence actually declined and his freedom of action was drastically curtailed by the State Department, which provided him with very specific instructions and left no room for personal initiative. Nor was Grew even informed of some of the important developments that took place in the course of the Hull-Nomura conversations. Ultimately, when Hull joined the "majority coalition" of Stimson and Morgenthau (while the president was becoming increasingly receptive to their persistent influence), Grew's only remaining option was "to shoot from the dark into the dark," as his images of Japan had no impact on the shaping of American Far Eastern policy (Iriye, 1973: 125).

The differences between Grew and Hull had to do with the two men's distinctive styles and approaches to politics. Whereas Grew was pragmatic and willing to compromise, Hull (while initially supporting a cautious strategy) had a strong dislike of compromise, insisting—on the very eve of the Pacific War—on the *immediate* implementation of *all* his policies as a prerequisite for a settlement with Japan. Grew's flexibility thus contrasted with Hull's basic tendency to subordinate specific controversial issues to the broader context of the ideological dichotomy between the "peace-loving, law-abiding nations and the aggressive, law-breaking nations."

President Roosevelt's occasional readiness to approve policies and decisions that directly contradicted his original recommendations is rather puzzling. He was confronted with pressures both from within his cabinet and from Chiang Kai-shek to oppose any compromise between the United States and Japan. Yet this cannot in itself justify Roosevelt's about-face in approving an aggressive proposal (Hull's Ten Point Plan) which had far-reaching ramifications for the future of American-Japanese relations. How could the President insist, on November 7, 1941, that American diplomacy "strain every nerve to satisfy and keep on good relations" with the Japanese negotiators, and then decide together with Hull, nearly three weeks later, "to kick the whole thing over" (Dallek, 1979: 305, 308)? What is particularly perplexing is that a decision of such magnitude (which sealed the fate of the Hull-Nomura negotiations) was made without any formal consultations with the military leadership (Langer and Gleason, 1953: 898).

Apparently, Roosevelt was unwilling to risk undermining the basic legitimation of his interventionist policy. Fearing that a major reorientation of American policy in the Pacific could well result in a substantial erosion in the public's support for his increasingly interventionist posture in Europe, he was reluctant to alienate the hard-liners in his cabinet, who played a leading role in the drive to move the nation away from isolationism. Roosevelt therefore decided to forgo his last-ditch efforts to replace the policy of coercion with one that was radically different.

No less striking is the facility with which Roosevelt abandoned his initial support for the proposed summit meeting with Konoye. An examination of the events between August 17, 1941, the day on which Nomura presented the proposal for the meeting, and October 2, 1941, the day on which Hull rejected the Japanese proposal de facto, indicates that the Japanese did not, in the interim, initiate any significant political or military move that might have been interpreted as incompatible with the proposal. On the contrary, seeking "to avoid war with the United States at any cost, even if it meant virtually nullifying the [Tripartite] Pact," Konoye initiated "an unmistakable shift in the Japanese position" (Hosoya, 1973: 161). This shift culminated in a new proposal (submitted to American negotiators on September 6) which asserted that "should the United States participate in the European war, the interpretation and execution of the Tripartite Pact shall be *independently* decided" (quoted in Hosoya, 1973: 161; italics in original).

This marked shift in the Japanese posture toward the United States was readily recognized by both Ambassador Grew (Hosoya, 1973: 161) and President Roosevelt. The latter's reaction to Konoye's letter of August 28 clearly reflects a conviction that the Japanese proposal was a sincere effort to break the diplomatic deadlock (U.S. Department of State, 1943: Vol. 2, Japan, 571–572). Even the British, who occasionally pressured the United States to adopt a firmer posture toward Japan, expressed a generally positive attitude toward Konoye's proposal. In the words of Sir Robert Craigie, the British ambassador to Tokyo (quoted in Kubek, 1965: 16), "It would [have been] a foolish policy if this superb opportunity [had been] permitted to slip by assuming an unduly suspicious attitude."

It appears that President Roosevelt's reversal in this case stemmed mainly from a single factor, namely, Hull's strong opposition. Roosevelt was, however, aware that "newspaper, public, and official opinion was uniformly opposed to any appeasement of Japan" and thus was also motivated by a reluctance to initiate unpopular courses of action (Dallek, 1979: 302). In retrospect, was the president justified in abandoning his original views in the face of this opposition? Although there is no clear-cut evidence that Konoye could have actually persuaded the leaders of the Japanese army to accept a modus vivendi agreement, it is equally uncertain that a compromise settlement acceptable to both the Roosevelt administration and the Japanese army was beyond reach.

As Jones (1954: 459) argues, the United States and Japan were not confronted in August 1941 with an absolute choice between a comprehensive settlement and an open conflict. The possibility of a modus vivendi settling some issues and leaving others in abeyance, still existed. Had Roosevelt and Konoye met, they might have agreed on a relaxation of the embargo in exchange for satisfactory assurances regarding Japan's future attitude toward the Tripartite Pact, at the same time brushing aside the China issue. According to this scenario, the United States would not have been forced to cut off aid to China, nor would Japan have been compelled to remove all her troops from China forthwith. The final settlement of such controversial issues as the question of China could have thus been postponed, pending the outcome of the war in Europe. Jones concludes:

> If Germany prevailed, then the U.S. would be in no position to oppose Japanese ambitions in Asia; if Germany were defeated, Japan would be in no position to persist in those ambitions in face of the U.S., the U.S.S.R. and the British Commonwealth.

> Konoye and the Court party did not want to persist in them be-
> cause their achievement would have meant the consolidation of
> the political predominance of the Army in Japan, to which the
> Court party were opposed, but which they dared not yet openly
> attack. (1954: 459)

According to this analysis, a modus vivendi settlement with Japan,
based on the convergence of American and Japanese interests, could
have resolved some of the most pressing issues, while the other controversial but less urgent questions could have been either set aside or at
least partially resolved during the following months. A prime factor
that could have facilitated this process of accommodation was the impact of developments on the German-Soviet front (such as the ultimate
failure of the German offensive of December 1941) on Japan's foreign
policy. Had an agreement been reached, it could have created a breath-
ing space for Japan, enabling her to assess the significance of Germany's
setbacks in her eastern campaign (Feis, 1950: 274–277; Schroeder, 1958:
208–209). In the same vein, Butow remarks:

> In the Hull-Nomura conversations, one dreary week had passed
> into another over a period of months without small successes
> along the way to sustain belief in the possibility of a settlement.
> . . . Something was needed to provoke the negotiators into at-
> tempting new approaches. A presidential decision to meet with
> the premier of Japan at Honolulu (or anywhere else for that
> matter) might have served as the necessary stimulus. . . . A
> Konoye-Roosevelt meeting could have been used to explore the
> diplomatic opportunities created by an expansion of the war in
> Europe [i.e., the Nazi attack on Soviet Russia] that had been un-
> dertaken by Hitler without regard for his Japanese allies, who
> shared a Neutrality Pact with the Russians. . . . Diplomacy is a
> nation's last line of defense short of war. There are times when
> personal contact between the highest political leaders of the
> contending sides can encourage decisions that protracted discus-
> sions at lower levels of competence and responsibility might not
> otherwise produce. It is difficult to believe that an abortive tête-
> à-tête would have resulted in any irreparable damage to the U.S.
> or that failure at Honolulu would have led to a graver interna-
> tional crisis than the one already in existence. (1972: 69–72)

In conclusion, the haste and facility with which President Roosevelt decided to abandon his initial support for the Japanese proposal for a summit meeting is indeed puzzling. Since both the army and the American embassy in Tokyo were excluded from the decision-making process leading to that decision, Hull's skepticism about the prospects of the proposed meeting (which was buttressed by the hard-liners' opposition to any step that could lead to a modus vivendi) was the only factor to prevail. With Roosevelt's attention diffused among many other issues, Hull managed to "talk the President out of his impulses and ideas" (Schroeder, 1958: 202), insisting, in his August 28, 1941, meeting with Nomura (U.S. Department of State, 1943: Vol. 2, Japan, 576), on a preliminary agreement regarding at least some of the controversial issues as a prerequisite for holding the summit meeting (even though the idea of the summit meeting had been proposed in light of the parties' inability to reach an initial, partial agreement). Hull was convinced that "serious consequences from the point of view of both Governments . . . would ensue if the meeting failed to result in an agreement as a consequence of issues arising which could not be resolved," and in his August 28 meeting with Nomura expressed the view "that the meeting should therefore have as its purpose the ratification of essential points already agreed to in principle" (U.S. Department of State, 1943: Vol. 2, Japan; 576–577). Therefore, President Roosevelt informed Ambassador Nomura, on September 3, 1941 (U.S. Department of State, 1943: Vol. 2, Japan; 588), that while "he was still favorable to a conference, it was very important to settle a number of these questions beforehand, if the success of the conference was to be safeguarded to the extent warranted by the holding of such a meeting."

As in the case of several other presidential decisions of the same period, Roosevelt's acceptance of Hull's position reflected his determination to ensure and legitimate his interventionist strategy, and thus to avoid at all costs antagonizing the proponents of this posture, whose support was vital in the struggle against the forces of isolationism. Ultimately, Hull's recommendation to, in effect, reject Konoye's proposal proved to be the decisive factor that sealed the fate of Konoye's moderate cabinet. While General Tojo, who succeeded Konoye in October, continued for a while to support the policy pursued by his predecessor, it is clear in retrospect that the failure of Konoye's initiative significantly weakened the bargaining position of the moderate leaders in Tokyo (Welles, 1944: 295). The latter were left empty-handed in their struggle against the militant officers within the army's general staff who favored war.

NOTES

1. The Reverend Malcolm Peabody was the son of the Reverend Endicott Peabody, who had been the headmaster of Groton school when Roosevelt was a student there during the period 1896–1899.

2. The president could not remember the exact term used by his Japanese friend to describe the nature of the "Japanese dynasty." According to Stimson (diary entry of May 17, 1934), "He [the Japanese friend] used a word indicating a rather fatherly control, which the President said he could not quite recall."

3. Interestingly, several members of Japan's policy elite held similar views regarding the limits of and dangers inherent in the unmitigated pursuit by Japan of a coercive political and military posture in the Pacific. For example, addressing the Imperial Conference on September 19, 1940, Privy Council President Yoshimichi Hara expressed opposition to the proposed Tripartite Pact, fearing that far from deterring the United States, the agreement was bound to further aggravate the already tense American-Japanese relations. As he pointed out in his cryptic statement:

> It seems to me that while the United States is playing the self-styled role of watchman in East Asia in place of Britain and is applying pressure upon Japan, still it refrains from extreme measures in order not to force Japan into joining the German-Italian side. However, once this Pact is made public and the Japanese attitude becomes clear, the United States will, I am afraid, greatly intensify its pressure upon Japan and increase its aid to Chiang in order to interfere with Japan's prosecution of the war. Furthermore, the United States, which has not declared war against Germany and Italy, will further intensify its economic pressure upon Japan without declaring war. It will apply measures of attrition against Japan by embargoing oil and iron and boycotting Japanese goods, so that Japan will not be able to carry on the war. . . . America is a proud nation. I am afraid that a firm attitude on our part may produce an adverse result. (Hosoya, 1976: 246–247)

SEVEN

Cordell Hull: The Idealistic Approach

The preceding pages have already touched upon the role played by Secretary of State Hull in formulating U.S. policy toward Japan. This chapter will systematize the various facets of Hull's contribution to the decision-making process. Whereas such hard-liners as Secretaries Stimson and Morgenthau approached Japan in terms of certain balance-of-power considerations, Secretary of State Cordell Hull's basic images of Japan were closely patterned on his legal-idealistic vision of the international system (George, 1980: 246; Dallek, 1983: 117). Hull was fully committed to humanitarian-universalist principles, and was thus ideologically predisposed to resent any power—including Japan—which "had no respect for the principles of international law" (Borg, 1964: 96; Thomson, 1973: 86; Pelz, 1974: 173). Despite this animosity, Hull, during most of the period preceding the war, continued to hope that moral education and persuasion, rather than coercion, could precipitate change in Japan's patterns of behavior on the international scene.

Thus while the posture recommended by the hard-liners was derived from their strategic (balance-of-power) perspective, Hull's basic approach to the Far Eastern crisis reflected his continued preoccupation with the Wilsonian concept of substituting international authority for national power, collective security for the national use of force and old-type alliances, and the rule of law in international affairs for the supremacy of the sovereign state (Pratt, 1964: 286–289; Thomson, 1973: 87, Pelz, 1974: 73). While both Hull and the hard-liners shared a basic animosity toward Japan, these similar images of Japan (as an inherently aggressive entity) were incorporated into different worldviews. Stimson, Morgenthau, and Hornbeck viewed Japan as an active participant in the worldwide revisionist drive to disrupt the global balance of power; Hull's image of Japan was integrated into a global dichotomy between those powers seeking remedies for grievances through strictly legal and peaceful means, and those—including Japan—which had no intention of abiding by international treaties.

Hull was a "Southern Democrat and Wilsonian, [who] revered high principles in personal and international conduct" (Thomson, 1973: 85; see also Borg, 1964: 96–97) and believed in general observance of such rules of morality as "noninterference in the internal affairs of other nations, peaceful settlement of controversies, observance of treaty obligations, and respect for international law" (Pratt, 1964: 30). He had no sympathy for any power which in his view failed to abide by these concepts (Pelz, 1974: 73). He adhered to "moral abstractions and principles," which he considered to be (1948: Vol. 1, 536) "as vital in international relations as the Ten Commandments in personal relations." He was incensed over Japan's refusal to remain within the framework of the system of collective security (Osgood, 1953: 362). Indeed, such events as Japan's departure from the League of Nations and her disregard for the Open Door policy helped establish in Hull's mind a clear-cut dichotomy between Japan, Fascist Italy, and Nazi Germany on the one hand, and the "remainder of the world community" which continued to seek remedies for grievances through strictly legal and peaceful means, on the other (Hull, 1948: Vol. 1, 270–271; also Borg, 1964: 96–97; Thomson, 1973: 100).

In Hull's view, since the latter half of the nineteenth century Japan as a power had displayed a cynical approach toward international agreements. He observed in his memoirs:

> She warred against China in 1894 in order to get hold of Korea. She fought Russia in 1904 and obtained Russia's lease of the Liatong Peninsula in Manchuria and a transfer to herself of the South Manchuria and other railways. She took advantage of the Western powers' absorption in the First World War to present her notorious twenty-one demands against China, which would have given her control of China. She declared war against Germany solely to get possession of German concessions in China and islands in the Pacific. She tried to annex Siberia east of Lake Baikal while Russia was engrossed in the Soviet Revolu-

tion. . . . As I entered the State Department, I had two points on
the Far East firmly in mind. One was the definite interest the
United States had in maintaining the independence of China and
in preventing Japan from gaining overlordship of the entire Far
East. The other was an equally definite conviction that Japan
had no intention whatever of abiding by treaties but would regulate her conduct by the opportunities of the moment. (1948: Vol.
1, 270–271)

During the period 1940–1941, these images of Japan were fully evident in Hull's approach toward the Far Eastern crisis. For example, in his
conversation with Ambassador Nomura (held on March 8, 1941), Hull assumed, according to Butow (1974: 28), "the aspect of a man who was trying to be both judge and prosecutor in a courtroom in which later gen-
erations would sit as the jury." Speaking with moral vigor and conviction, he pointed out that

with Japanese military forces clambering all over China, with
Japanese troops and ships and aircraft operating as far south as
French Indochina and Thailand, accompanied by such threatening declarations as Japanese statesmen were in the habit of making week after week, nations that were vitally interested in see-
ing world conquest and barbaric methods of government brought
to a halt could not but become increasingly concerned. *If Japan
could prove that she intended in good faith to abandon expansion
through force, all would be well. Nothing would be gained, however, if
Japan's military leaders were to make new avowals now only to break
them later on, as they had so frequently done in the past.* (U.S.
Department of State, 1943: Vol. 2, Japan, 393; italics added; see
also Butow, 1974: 29)

Similarly, in his June 2, 1941, meeting with Nomura, Hull inquired

whether Japan really is seeking [a settlement for peace and non-
discriminatory commercial relations and friendship in the Pa-
cific], or whether she is only seeking . . . to go forward with
methods and practices entirely contrary to the principles which
would have to underlie a settlement establishing peace, non-
discriminatory commerce and fair relations in the Pacific area.
(U.S. Department of State, 1943: Vol. 2, Japan, 454–455)

Nevertheless, Hull's sharply delineated, pre-existing visions of Japan and of the international system did not always impel him into a coercive posture in the Pacific. Thus, whereas the hard-liners continued to support comprehensive economic sanctions as the only means of restraining Japan, Hull, being an essentially cautious man, realized that an intransigent posture could well lead to escalation (Pelz, 1974: 73). Consequently, he opposed, though with an ever-diminishing enthusiasm, the uncompromising policy advocated by Stimson, Morgenthau, and Hornbeck. In the words of Anderson:

> Within the American government . . . restraint came almost exclusively from the Department of State. . . . Even though his lieutenants had become restive, Hull was determined [in 1940] to avoid provocations that might result in a Japanese descent on the Indies, and in this course he had the firm support of the President. Behind the floodwall, however, pressure for more vigorous action had been building in several other agencies. (1975: 168)

In George's terminology (1969: passim), despite Hull's philosophical beliefs, which reflected an irreconcilable animosity toward the Japanese opponent, he was motivated—on the instrumental, practical level—by a cluster of constraints which dictated a patient and reserved operational code.

The dangers inherent in a policy of harsh economic sanctions against Japan were recognized by Hull as early as November 1937. He was aware that this policy might provoke "a war for which the United States was unprepared," and thus rejected the demands raised by the members of the American delegation to the Brussels conference for "some form of pressure upon Japan." Following the *Panay* incident of December 1937, Hull similarly objected to Morgenthau's attempts to establish an Anglo-American bloc designed to pursue an uncompromising policy toward Japan (Pratt, 1964: 451).

Three years later, on December 2, 1940 (appearing before the Senate Committee on Banking and Currency), Hull again warned of the dangers of pursuing an irreconcilable posture toward Japan. He began his analysis of the Far Eastern situation (see a memorandum on Hull's appearance before the committee in *The Morgenthau Diary*, 1940: Book 334, December 1–2) by depicting a worldwide dichotomy between the "peace-loving nations" and "those nations which have been proceeding ruthlessly to walk across the face of the world, without warning or justifications, and breaking whatever laws they please." However, when the committee turned to the more concrete issue of economic sanctions, Hull's vigor and decisiveness quickly faded. "The question of whether or not to impose a total embargo on exports to Japan," he told the committee, "was a very delicate matter, and we had been maneuvering as carefully as possible without getting directly into trouble." Hull's caution and initial reluctance to support drastic economic sanctions were repeatedly criticized by Stimson, who on several occasions during 1940 expressed disappointment at the "inaction of the State Department." For example, on May 8, Stimson remarked in his diary (1939–1940: Vol. 29, January 1939– June 25, 1940) that "Hull, for various reasons, does not grasp and lead his own Department quite as thoroughly as I think he should." On November 1, Stimson again complained in his diary (1940: Vol. 31, October 1, 1940–November 30) of the "timidity which seems to be prevalent in the State Department and which has resulted in a good deal of inaction in the Far East."

Hull's basic caution as well as his "aversion to a showdown" in the Pacific (Burns, 1970: 136) were reinforced by his belief in the innate human capacity to undergo drastic behavioral transformation. Thus, despite his "devil theory of Japanese politics" (Burns, 1970: 136), he still retained some hope that the vicious cycle of mutual suspicion could be broken by "moral education" and persuasion.

A clear illustration of this dimension in Hull's thinking is found in his remarks to Ambassador Nomura, made during their meeting of April 14, 1941. The secretary of state, who was a "model of circumspection" (Butow, 1974: 161), elaborated during the course of this encounter on "the improvement that had taken place in recent years in Pan-American relations," maintaining that this positive development was "an illustration of what could be achieved if only the nations of the world would agree to abide by certain fundamental principles in their conduct toward each other" (quoted in Butow, 1974: 161–162).

Not until the summer of 1941 was this propensity for an essentially restrained posture toward Japan finally modified. Then, the impact of the constant pressures exerted by the hard-liners, combined with Hull's growing frustration with the apparent failure of his preferred strategy of inducing the Japanese, through moral persuasion, to change their operational code in the Pacific, finally outweighed his initial caution. The turning point in Hull's thinking occurred in the wake of Japan's occupation of naval and air bases in southern Indochina. Hull was

angered by this move, as it signaled to him the inadequacy of the restrained approach which he had hitherto supported (Divine, 1965: 121).
He therefore decided, on July 23, 1941, to temporarily suspend his negotiations with Ambassador Nomura, and to give his support to the "freezing order" of July 25. According to Stimson's account (quoted in Anderson, 1975: 189), Hull returned to Washington on August 4 (from White
Sulphur Springs) convinced that the United States had "reached the end
of possible appeasement with Japan and there is nothing further that
can be done with that country except by a firm policy."

Hull's feelings of total disillusionment in the aftermath of the "Indochina crisis" surfaced most clearly during his conversation with Sumner
Welles. He averred: "They [the Japanese] swear every day that they are
going forward and they are fitting their acts to their words." But he
added:

> The only time they modify their policy of overt, unfriendly acts
> is when they make false and fraudulent avowals of peace and
> friendship. This they do until they get ready to go forward
> [again]. . . . *Nothing will stop them except force.* Unless we figure
> that they are going to turn back, we should not figure that they
> are going to be satisfied to stop where they are. The point is how
> long we can maneuver the situation until the military matter in
> Europe is brought to a conclusion. (quoted in Butow, 1974: 241;
> italics added)

This change in Hull's thinking was instantly recognized by Stimson,
who observed (quoted in Butow, 1974: 241): "He [Hull] has made up his
mind that we have reached the end of any possible appeasement with
Japan and that there is nothing further that can be done with that
country except by a firm policy."

Ultimately, then, it was the alliance between the humanistic-
universalist vision of the world, represented by Hull, and the balance-
of-power approach, represented by the hard-liners, combined with the
president's growing readiness to acquiesce and support the "majority
coalition," which tipped the scale in favor of the advocates of an uncompromising posture toward Japan. The desire of Stimson, Morgenthau, and Hornbeck to prevent the disruption of the global balance
of power thus merged with Hull's growing readiness to set aside his preferred strategy of persuasion and moral education for the sake of vigorously opposing the forces which, in his view, threatened to under-

mine the system of collective security based on international law (Iriye, 1967: 222). Hull's decision to incorporate his general, abstract principles into a *short-term* political scheme, namely, the "Ten Point Plan" (which insisted on the immediate and unconditional implementation of *all* the American principles in the Pacific and was originally drafted by the Treasury Department) made him, at long last, a natural partner to the hard-line coalition, and thus further aggravated a tense situation.

Indeed, during the early phase of the Hull-Nomura conversations, the secretary of state adopted an incremental approach which sought "to argue Japan into modifying here, eliminating there, and inserting elsewhere, until we might reach an accord we both could sign with mutual good will" (Hull's words of May 1941, quoted in Butow, 1974: 185–186), and in November 1941 he approved and presented to the Japanese a plan ("the Ten Point Plan") which was "final in character." In Schroeder's words,

> First, the proposal [the Ten Point Plan] was unprecedented. No doubt Hull and his associates always considered the ten points, or something like them, to be an ideal solution of Asiatic problems. But never before had they been presented as demands to Japan in so bold and sweeping a fashion. . . . Second, the Ten Point Plan was one-sided. While most of the proposals [incorporated into the plan] were indeed mutual in form, they were completely unconciliatory and uncompromising in reality. (1958: 88)

EIGHT

Synthesis and Conclusion: The Worldview, the Image, and the Shaping of American Policy Toward Japan

As we have sought to demonstrate, the individuals involved in the shaping of the U.S. Pacific policy in 1940–1941 constituted a heterogeneous group. Although most of them shared a number of concepts which were integrated into their respective worldviews, they differed in the relative weight which they accorded these concepts. As a result of these differing perceptions, there were unbridgeable gaps between the policies promulgated by one group and those advocated by another.

For example, while both Secretary Hull and Ambassador Grew believed that the same "fundamental principles" should be "universally adopted and maintained," their views differed widely regarding the relative importance of these ideological considerations in formulating

The following analysis incorporates, builds upon, and occasionally modifies some of the ideas in Ben-Zvi (1975: 230–239). I wish to thank Professor Akira Iriye for his insightful suggestions concerning the typologies advanced in this chapter.

specific policy recommendations toward Japan. Hull and Grew both recognized the need "to maintain and protect the vital interests of the U.S.," yet they sharply disagreed, particularly during the period immediately preceding the war, as to whether or not narrowly defined considerations of "national interest" should be given priority over ideological premises. Hence, whereas Grew strongly supported the proposed American-Japanese modus vivendi agreement (which would have required the United States to temporarily set aside or even sacrifice certain principles for the sake of averting an immediate war in the Pacific), Hull's ideological preconceptions eventually overshadowed all other considerations, leading him to oppose the various modus vivendi drafts which did not fully conform to all his principles.

Based on the foregoing analysis, two typologies emerge. These are designed to categorize, in terms of both content and structure, the divergent images and belief systems, as well as the preferred strategies, held by the various individuals within the Roosevelt administration. It is hoped that by integrating the main findings of this case study into this twofold analytical grouping, we shall establish a more comprehensive, multifaceted picture of the cognitive (as well as political and bureaucratic) processes which profoundly influenced the shaping of American diplomacy in the Pacific—and which may also be relevant in other crisis situations.

The first typology distinguishes among the actors involved in the decision-making process in terms of their *predominant* images of the world and of the unfolding crisis in the Pacific in 1940 and 1941. These divergent perceptions precipitated certain incompatible policy recommendations toward Japan, which were occasionally translated into reality. The relative power, bargaining skill, level of motivation, and resolve of the various actors, combined with the availability, to some of them, of certain bureaucratic resources, were the main factors which determined the extent to which images became the source of American policy in the Pacific.

In these terms the individuals engaged in the formulation of the American posture toward Japan can be divided into three groups, which may be called (a) the globalist-realists, (b) the globalist-idealists, and (c) the nationalist-pragmatists.

The globalist-realists included Secretaries Stimson and Morgenthau as well as advisor Hornbeck. (Secretary Ickes may also be considered a globalist-realist policy maker, although he differed from the other members of the group in believing that war in the Pacific was inevitable, and that, consequently, the United States should be the first to strike. Ickes's thinking was also shaped by a cluster of idealistic-liberal considerations.) These policy makers perceived American national interests in the Far East as but one element within the worldwide effort initiated by Germany, Italy, and Japan to disrupt the global balance of power and thereby threaten the security of the United States. Convinced that events halfway around the globe had an automatic, direct impact on America's core interests, the globalist-realist decision makers were thus predisposed to view any adverse turn of events anywhere as endangering the United States (Friedmann, 1968: 174; Ben-Zvi, 1975: 231; 1981: 388–389).

The globalist-realist insistence on such parameters of national security precluded any attempt to analyze the Pacific crisis on its own terms. The regional events which took place in the Pacific in 1940 and 1941 were perceived as but one facet of a larger pattern, whose significance lay beyond the regional boundaries within which they unfolded, and whose particular characteristics went ignored. This proclivity by Stimson, Morgenthau, and Hornbeck to assimilate local occurrences into universal frameworks inevitably led them, therefore, to view any perceived adversary—including Japan—as an integral part of the developing conspiracy to encroach upon America's security (see in this connection, the definition of the "fixed-sum game" in Schelling, 1960). Indeed, once Japan was viewed by the globalist-realists as being an organic part of the highly cohesive revisionist coalition, the general attributes of all coalition forces of change were applied to her. Japan was therefore perceived as being an inherently aggressive power in a "closed" international system (Ben Zvi, 1981: 391; see also, in this connection, Friedmann, 1968: 174; Holsti, 1979: 343; Lanir, 1981: 6).

In addition to this globalist-realist propensity to perceive the political-strategic environment as a "closed system," the attitude of Stimson and Hornbeck in 1940–1941 was further affected by certain past events and experiences which provided the source of future perceptions and analogies, and were fully integrated into a dichotomous, highly conflictual worldview. During the period immediately preceding the war, these sharply delineated visions of the international system led the globalist-realists to assimilate and interpret incoming information in a way which conformed with and reinforced their pre-existing background images. This further precipitated a congruent, hard-line strategy (except in the case of Ickes) which sought to *deter* Japan with comprehensive economic sanctions.

By virtue of its continued insistence· on an uncompromising posture, this group of policy makers fully corresponds with what Snyder and Diesing (1977: 302–303) describe as the "hard-line" type of political actors. The typical hard-liner views the opponent as "systematically expansionist, with unlimited aims," and tends to advocate "firm deterrence [as] the only appropriate strategy." It was precisely this intransigent policy which was implemented by the United States on the eve of Pearl Harbor.

Whereas the globalist-realists held the "sphere of influence" view, which assumed that American national security would be guaranteed by the balance of power, Secretary of State Cordell Hull is a clear illustration of a globalist-idealist policy maker. Hull was fully committed to an idealistic-universalist vision of the world which was predicated upon such principles as the sanctity of treaties and "peaceful change." Perceiving the international system in terms of moral rather than strategic categories, Hull was deeply devoted to a utopian vision of the future international system, in which "there will no longer be need for spheres of influence, for balance of power, or any other of the special arrangements through which, in the unhappy past, the nations strove to safeguard their security or to promote their interests" (quoted in Schlesinger, 1967: 27). (While the thinking of Secretary Ickes also incorporated idealistic elements, his aggressive tactics and advocacy of a military strike against Japan set him apart from Hull, whose original approach was cautious and restrained.)

Unlike the globalist-realists, whose image of Japan was incorporated into the vision of the mounting threat to the balance of power, Hull's perception of Japan was integrated into a global dichotomy between "those powers which continuously sought remedies for grievances through strictly legal and peaceful means" and those national entities which—lacking any intention of "abiding by treaties"—tended to "regulate their conduct by the opportunities of the moment" (Hull, 1948: Vol. 1, 270–271; see also Borg, 1964: 96–97; Thomson, 1973: 100). However, viewing himself as a moral educator, Hull was *initially* more optimistic than Stimson, Morgenthau, and Hornbeck regarding the prospects of reforming—through continued persuasion—Japan's modus operandi in the Pacific.

It was only in the aftermath of the Japanese invasion of southern Indochina that this original gap between the cautious posture advocated by Hull and the more aggressive, uncompromising policy favored by the globalist-realists was finally bridged. The secretary of state became increasingly disillusioned with the apparent failure of his persistent educational effort to induce the Japanese to radically modify their approach to the Pacific crisis, and continued to be faced with a powerful and cohesive globalist-realist bloc. Thus Hull, as well as the president, ultimately decided to set aside his reservations and to give support to the maximalistic strategy of the globalist-realists.

The third group of policy makers may be labeled "nationalist-pragmatists." This group included President Roosevelt and Ambassador Grew, as well as a number of army and navy officers. The nationalist-pragmatists perceived the question of American-Japanese relations in 1940 and 1941 within the delimited framework of the "maintenance and protection of American national interests." The members of this group were acutely aware of the likely repercussions of an Axis victory in Europe, and viewed this as far more dangerous to U.S. security than further Japanese incursions to the south. Fearing that a coercive strategy might precipitate rather than prevent a conflagration in the Pacific, they recommended an accommodative, flexible policy toward Japan. Whereas the globalist-realists tended to perceive American national security as an all-inclusive, limitless concept (and therefore to incorporate any regional disturbance into a worldwide, highly threatening complex), the nationalist-pragmatists advocated a "limitationist position," based upon the notion that only those crises which posed an immediate threat to a narrowly defined cluster of vital interests should motivate the United States to act resolutely (Ben-Zvi, 1981: 389; see also, in this connection, Roskin, 1974: 567; Rochester, 1978: 48–58). Given this reluctance to automatically apply to the local theater certain preconceived global concepts and interpretations, it becomes clear why there was such a fundamental gap between the policies initially advocated by these two groups.

However, the globalist-realists formed a united front whose members were fully committed to the same basic perceptions, while the nationalist-pragmatists (who were partially and temporarily supported by the globalist-idealist Hull) constituted a heterogeneous "blocking coalition" whose two most prominent members, Roosevelt and Grew, differed from each other in terms of both their background images of Japan and their relative degree of resolve. Grew's accommodative posture was derived from his basic soft-line image of Japan, and as such he deeply empathized with the Japanese. In contrast, Roosevelt's initial moderation came solely from a cluster of pragmatic considerations which formed his "immediate images" of the escalating crisis.

   The president was essentially a pragmatist, who was occasionally willing to deviate from the Wilsonian tradition to which he belonged in
principle (Schlesinger, 1967: 26–27). He was thus predisposed to set aside,
at least temporarily, his background images of Japan for the sake of
reaching a modus vivendi in the Pacific and thereby averting an unnecessary confrontation. But this central (and formally most powerful)
decision maker—both in the group and in the entire decision-making
machinery—lacked the necessary resolve to carry out his preferred strategy, while the highly motivated Grew was deprived of any influence in
the shaping of American diplomacy. This contributed to the ultimate
failure of the nationalist-pragmatist coalition in the bureaucratic struggle over the formulating of American policy toward Japan. Secretary
of State Hull, who initially backed some of the policies recommended by
the nationalist-pragmatists, also did not persist in his cautious approach.
Like the president, he was ultimately persuaded by the globalist-realists
to give support to their preferred course of action.
   Given this asymmetry in the level of motivation between the two major representatives of the pragmatic-nationalist type of policy maker, it
is hardly surprising that it was the globalist-realist group, with its high
resolve to carry out its recommended policy, which managed to win most
of the decision games which in 1940–1941 divided the Roosevelt
administration. Some of the early victories of this faction in the course
of cabinet meetings (such as that of July 19, 1940) were incomplete when
viewed separately, and by no means satisfied Stimson and Morgenthau.
However, when taken in the aggregate, these victories had a profound
impact on the shaping of American policy toward Japan even before the
presidential decision of July 25, 1941, which froze all Japanese assets in
the United States.
   The various members of Roosevelt's policy elite were not equally
committed to their group's dominant worldview. Nor did similar visions
of the world and of the Japanese opponent necessarily trigger identical
policy recommendations. Based upon this structural distinction, the
second typology categorizes the members of the Roosevelt entourage in
terms of the extent to which they adhered to their original background
images.
   Specifically, following the analysis of Snyder and Diesing (1977:
325–339), two types of decision makers can be identified: (a) the open
(or rational) structural type, and (b) the closed (or irrational) structural type. The open type of decision maker, which is most clearly
represented by President Roosevelt, is characterized by his conceptual

flexibility and occasional willingness to decouple—within the confines of the Far Eastern crisis—his immediate behavior patterns from his pre-existing, fundamental images of the adversary. Indeed, Roosevelt was sensitive to his opponent's "overt statements and actions," and tended to base his information processing not on what he "knew" the Japanese "fundamental characteristics and ultimate aims were," but rather on the "developing pattern of information itself" (Snyder and Diesing, 1977: 333–335). As a result, his preconceived images of the Japanese adversary as an inherently aggressive entity gradually subsided into the background in the course of the crisis, and were overshadowed by a cluster of immediate images which reflected the president's doubts as to whether his initial images were at all relevant within the delimited context of American-Japanese relations in 1940–1941. Roosevelt was convinced that Japanese policy did not reflect any fixed plans for unlimited expansion and that the Japanese were "having a real drag-down and knock-out fight among themselves" regarding the course of action to be followed in the Pacific. Hence he supported, during most of the period preceding the war, an accomodative strategy which was incompatible with his basic perceptions of the Japanese opponent. This strategy did, however, reflect his revulsion at the possibility of a Pacific conflagration, for which the United States was ill-prepared.

By comparison, the closed (or irrational) type of decision maker, which is most clearly represented by the "two extremes" of Secretary Ickes on the one hand and Bishop Walsh and Father Drought on the other (as well as by the globalist-realists), is characterized by a rigid belief system which always dominates behavior. Irrevocably committed to their basic, pre-existing visions of the world, these closed (or irrational) policy makers were therefore predisposed, from the onset of the American-Japanese crisis, to interpret all new information solely "by means of the image" (Snyder and Diesing, 1977: 331–338). Ickes (the ultra-hard-liner), Stimson, Morgenthau, and Hornbeck, who were the hard-line globalist-realists, and Walsh and Drought, the ultra-soft-liners, believed that their fundamental perceptions provided the *only* basis of knowledge and tended to either reinterpret or ignore discrepant information. Indeed, while some of the closed policy makers differed widely from one another in terms of the specific *content* of the policy they advocated, they nonetheless shared an essentially similar *structure* of respective belief systems.

Still, that several members of Washington's policy elite upheld their initial images and were highly motivated to convert them into congruent policies could not in itself guarantee that these images would indeed have major behavioral ramifications. For example, for all his determined efforts, Ambassador Grew (who can be thought of as a relatively closed, soft-line nationalist-pragmatist) was severely constrained, and ultimately totally unsuccessful, in his drive to redirect American diplomacy in accordance with his basic perceptions. On the other hand, Stimson and Morgenthau ultimately managed to translate their pre-existing visions into derivative political decisions of great magnitude. In this sense, it was only when they were backed and reinforced by such political and administrative assets as bargaining skill, proximity to the central decision maker, and control over organizational resources that initial images proved to be instrumental in both precipitating governmental policies and shaping the reality of American-Japanese relations.

However, that the globalist-realists succeeded in inextricably linking fundamental perceptions to official policy lines should by no means imply that these images were accurate, that is, that they fully corresponded to what is defined by Brecher (1972) as "the operational environment." In fact, various policies (as well as interpretations of specific political developments) which were closely patterned on basic images of Japan held by members of this group were grossly mistaken, and reflected the gap which sometimes separated the "psychological environment" from the real world.

In this vein, the study of American images of Japan before Pearl Harbor is a study of convictions that failed to correspond to reality; of ideas tenaciously adhered to by a few men in defiance of a recalcitrant world.

There is no panacea that would render policy elites totally immune to the ever-present danger of misperception (Wohlstetter, 1962: 397–401; Handel, 1976: 62–64; Jervis, 1976: 409–424; Betts, 1982). Still, it is hoped that the foregoing analysis will help political actors, who constantly confront uncertain and threatening situations, to recognize that what may appear to them as self-evident and unambiguous inferences often only seem so because of their pre-existing beliefs, and may have no intrinsic validity (Jervis, 1968: 462).

Thus, if there is one central lesson which emerges from this case study, it is the need to recognize the inherently biased and subjective nature of our images and theories. One can indeed hope that this reconstruction of the conceptual origins of a traumatic conflagration, which neither the United States nor Japan sought, will highlight the need for a greater awareness of the difficulties inherent in the decision maker's constant confrontation with ambiguous and often conflicting stimuli.

Bibliography

Allison, Graham T. 1971. *Essence of Decision: Explaining the Cuban Missile Crisis.* Boston: Little, Brown.

Anderson, Irvine H., Jr. 1975. *The Standard-Vacuum Oil Company and United States East Asian Policy, 1933–1941.* Princeton: Princeton University Press.

Barnes, Harry Elmor, ed. 1953. *Perpetual War for Perpetual Peace.* Caldwell, Idaho: Caxton.

Beard, Charles A. 1948. *President Roosevelt and the Coming of War, 1941.* New Haven: Yale University Press.

Bemis, S. F. 1948. The First Gun of a Revisionist Historiography for the Second World War. *Journal of Modern History* 19 (March): 55–59.

Bentley, Arthur F. 1954. *Inquiry into Inquiries: Essays in Science Series.* Boston: Beacon Press.

Ben-Zvi, Abraham. 1975. American Preconceptions and Policies Toward Japan, 1940–1941: A Case Study in Misperception. *International Studies Quarterly* 19 (June): 228–248.

———. 1976. Hindsight and Foresight: A Conceptual Framework for the Analysis of Surprise Attacks. *World Politics* 28 (April): 381–395.

———. 1980. Perception, Action and Reaction: A Comparative Analysis of Decision-Making Processes in Bilateral Conflicts. *Journal of Political Science* 7 (Spring): 95–111.

———. 1981. In Pursuit of National Security: A Juxtaposition of American Images and Policies. *Journal of Strategic Studies* (December): 386–414.

Betts, Richard K. 1978. Analysis, War, and Decision. *World Politics* 31 (October): 61–89.

———. 1980–81. Surprise Despite Warning: Why Sudden Attacks Succeed. *Political Science Quarterly* 95 (Winter): 551–572.

————. 1982. *Surprise Attack: Lessons for Defense Planning.* Washington, D.C.: Brookings Institution.

Blum, John M. 1970. *Roosevelt and Morgenthau.* Boston: Houghton Mifflin.

Borg, Dorothy. 1964. *The United States and the Far Eastern Crisis of 1933–38: From the Manchurian Incident Through the Initial Stage of the Undeclared Sino-Japanese War.* Cambridge: Harvard University Press.

Borg, Dorothy, and Okamoto, Shumpei. eds. 1973. *Pearl Harbor as History: Japanese-American Relations, 1931–1941.* New York: Columbia University Press.

Boulding, Kenneth E. 1956. *The Image.* Ann Arbor: University of Michigan Press.

————. 1959. National Images and International Systems. *Journal of Conflict Resolution* 3 (June): 120–131.

Brecher, Michael. 1972. *The Foreign Policy System of Israel: Setting, Images, Process.* New Haven: Yale University Press.

Bronfenbrenner, Urie. 1961. The Mirror Image in Soviet-American Relations: A Social Psychologist's Report. *Journal of Social Issues* 17: 45–56.

Burns, James M. 1970. *Roosevelt: The Soldier of Freedom.* New York: Harcourt, Brace.

Butow, Robert J. C. 1960. The Hull-Nomura Conversations: A Fundamental Misconception. *American Historical Review* 65 (July): 822–836.

————. 1961. *Tojo and the Coming of War.* Princeton: Princeton University Press.

————. 1972. Backdoor Diplomacy in the Pacific: The Proposal for a Roosevelt-Konoye Meeting, 1941. *Journal of American History* 59 (June): 48–72.

————. 1974. *The John Doe Associates: Backdoor Diplomacy for Peace, 1941.* Stanford: Stanford University Press.

Chamberlin, William H. 1950. *America's Second Crusade.* Chicago: Regnery.

Cohen, Warren I. 1973. The Role of Private Groups in the United States. In *Pearl Harbor as History.* See Borg and Okamoto (1973).

————. 1978. *The Chinese Connection: Roger S. Greene, Thomas W. Lamont, George E. Sobolsky and American-East Asian Relations.* New York: Columbia University Press.

Cole, Wayne S. 1973. The Role of the United States Congress and Political Parties. In *Pearl Harbor as History.* See Borg and Okamoto (1973).

Current, Richard N. 1950. *Secretary Stimson: A Study in Statecraft.* New Brunswick, N.J.: Rutgers University Press.

Dallek, Robert. 1979. *Franklin D. Roosevelt and American Foreign Policy, 1932–1945.* New York: Oxford University Press.

———. 1983. *The American Style of Foreign Policy.* New York: Alfred A. Knopf.

DeConde, Alexander. 1963. *A History of American Foreign Policy.* New York: Scribner's.

DeSantis, Hugh. 1980. *The Diplomacy of Silence: The American Foreign Service, The Soviet Union, and the Cold War, 1933–1947.* Chicago: University of Chicago Press.

Divine, Robert A. 1962. *The Illusion of Neutrality.* Chicago: University of Chicago Press.

———. 1965. *The Reluctant Belligerent: American Entry into World War II.* New York: Wiley.

———. 1969. *Roosevelt and World War II.* Baltimore: Johns Hopkins University Press.

Eckstein, Harry. 1975. Case Studies and Theory in Political Science. In Fred I. Greenstein and Nelson W. Polsby (eds.), *Handbook of Political Science,* Vol. 7. Reading, Mass.: Addison-Wesley.

Emmerson, John K. 1978. *The Japanese Thread: A File in the U.S. Foreign Service.* New York: Holt, Rinehart and Winston.

Falkowski, Lawrence S. 1979. Predicting Flexibility with Memory Profiles. In Lawrence S. Falkowski (ed.), *Psychological Models in International Politics.* Boulder: Westview Press.

Fehrenbach, T. R. 1967. *F.D.R.'s Undeclared War: 1939–1941.* New York: David McKay.

Feis, Herbert. 1950. *The Road to Pearl Harbor.* Princeton: Princeton University Press.

———. 1956. War Came at Pearl Harbor: Suspicions Considered. *Yale Review* 45 (March): 378–390.

Friedländer, Saul. 1967. *Prelude to Downfall: Hitler and the United States, 1939–41.* New York: Alfred A. Knopf.

Friedmann, Wolfgang. 1968. Interventionism, Liberalism, and Power-Politics: The Unfinished Revolution in International Thinking. *Political Science Quarterly* 83 (June): 169–189.

Gardner, Lloyd. 1973. The Role of the Commerce and Treasury Departments. In *Pearl Harbor as History.* See Borg and Okamoto (1973).

George, Alexander L. 1969. The 'Operational Code': A Neglected Approach to the Study of Political Leaders and Decision-Making. *International Studies Quarterly* 13 (June): 190–221.

———. 1979a. The Causal Nexus Between Cognitive Beliefs and Decision-Making Behavior: The "Operational Code" Belief System. In *Psychological Models.* See Falkowski (1979).

———. 1979b. Case Studies and Theory Development: The Method of Structured, Focused Comparison. In *Diplomacy*. See Gordon (1979).

———. 1980. Domestic Constraints on Regime Change in U.S. Foreign Policy: The Need for Policy Legitimacy. In Ole R. Holsti, Randolph M. Siverson, and Alexander L. George (eds.), *Change in the International System*. Boulder: Westview Press.

George, Alexander L., and Smoke, Richard. 1974. *Deterrence in American Foreign Policy*. New York: Columbia University Press.

George, Alexander L., Hall, David K., and Simons, William E. 1971. *The Limits of Coercive Diplomacy: Laos, Cuba, Vietnam*. Boston: Little, Brown.

Graebner, Norman A. 1973. Hoover, Roosevelt, and the Japanese. In *Pearl Harbor as History*. See Borg and Okamoto (1973).

Greer, Thomas H. 1958. *What Roosevelt Thought: The Social and Political Ideas of Franklin D. Roosevelt*. East Lansing: Michigan State University.

Grew, Joseph C. 1952. *Turbulent Era: A Diplomatic Record of Forty Years, 1904–1945*. Boston: Houghton Mifflin.

Halperin, Morton. 1974. *Bureaucratic Politics and Foreign Policy*. Washington, D.C.: Brookings Institution.

Handel, Michael I. 1976. *Perception, Deception and Surprise: The Case of the Yom Kippur War* (Jerusalem Papers on Peace Problems, No. 19). Jerusalem: Leonard Davis Institute for International Relations, The Hebrew University, 1976.

Heinrichs, Waldo H., Jr. 1966. *American Ambassador: Joseph C. Grew and the Development of the United States Diplomatic Tradition*. Boston: Little, Brown.

———. 1973. The Role of the United States Navy. In *Pearl Harbor as History*. See Borg and Okamoto (1973).

Hermann, Margaret G. 1978. Effects of Personal Characteristics of Personal Leaders on Foreign Policy. In Maurice A. East, Stephen A. Salmore, and Charles F. Hermann (eds.), *Why Nations Act: Theoretical Perspectives for Comparative Foreign Policy Studies*. Beverly Hills, Calif.: Sage Publications.

Hoffmann, Stanley. 1968. *Gulliver's Troubles, or the Setting of American Foreign Policy*. New York: McGraw-Hill.

Hofstadter, Richard. 1957. *The American Political Tradition and the Men Who Made It*. New York: Alfred A. Knopf.

Holsti, Ole R. 1962. The Belief System and National Images: A Case Study. *Journal of Conflict Resolution* 6 (September): 244–251.

————. 1967. Cognitive Dynamics and Images of the Enemy: Dulles and Russia. In David J. Finlay, Ole R. Holsti, and Richard R. Fagen (eds.), *Enemies in Politics.* Chicago: Rand, McNally.

————. 1976. Foreign Policy Formation Viewed Cognitively. In Robert Axelrod (ed.), *Structure of Decision: The Cognitive Maps of Political Elites.* Princeton: Princeton University Press.

————. 1979. The Three-Headed Eagle: The United States and System Change, *International Studies Quarterly* 23 (September): 339–359.

————. 1982. The Operational Code Approach: Problems and Some Solutions. In Christer Jönsson (ed.), *Cognitive Dynamics and International Politics.* New York: St. Martin's.

Hooker, Nancy Harrison. 1965. *The Moffat Papers: Selections from the Diplomatic Journals of Jay Pierrpoint Moffat, 1919–1943.* Cambridge: Harvard University Press.

Hopkins, Harry L. 1935–1945. *Papers.* Hyde Park, N.Y.: Franklin D. Roosevelt Library.

Hopple, Gerald W., and Rossa, Paul J. 1981. International Crisis Analysis: Recent Developments and Future Directions. In P. Terrence Hopmann, Dina A. Zinnes, and J. David Singer (eds.), *Cumulation in International Relations Research.* Denver: Monograph Series in World Affairs, Vol. 18, Book 3.

Hornbeck, Stanley. 1916. *Contemporary Politics in the Far East.* New York.

Hosoya, Chihiro. 1968. Miscalculations in Deterrent Policy: Japanese-U.S. Relations, 1938–41. *Journal of Peace Research* 5 (Summer): 97–115.

————. 1973. The Role of Japan's Foreign Ministry and Its Embassy in Washington, 1940–1941. In *Pearl Harbor as History.* See Borg and Okamoto (1973).

————. 1974. Characteristics of the Foreign Policy Decision-Making System in Japan, *World Politics* 26 (April): 353–369.

————. 1976. The Tripartite Pact, 1939–1940. In James William Morley (ed.), *Deterrence Diplomacy: Japan, Germany, and the USSR, 1935–1940.* New York: Columbia University Press.

Hsu, Immanuel C. J. 1952. Kurusu's Mission to the United States and the Abortive *Modus Vivendi, Journal of Modern History* 24 (September): 301–307.

Hull, Cordell. 1948. *The Memoirs of Cordell Hull.* 2 vols. New York: Macmillan.

Ickes, Harold L. 1953–54. *The Secret Diary of Harold L Ickes.* 3 vols. New York: Simon and Schuster.

Irish, Marian D., and Elke, Frank. 1975. *U.S. Foreign Policy: Context, Conduct, Content.* New York: Harcourt, Brace.

Iriye, Akira. 1967. *Across the Pacific: An Inner History of American-Asian Relations.* New York: Harcourt, Brace.

———. 1973. The Role of the United States Embassy in Tokyo. In *Pearl Harbor as History.* See Borg and Okamoto (1973).

———. 1981. *Power and Culture: The Japanese-American War, 1941–1945.* Cambridge: Harvard University Press.

Janis, Irving L. 1972. *Victims of Groupthink.* Boston: Houghton Mifflin.

Jervis, Robert. 1968. Hypotheses on Misperception. *World Politics* 20 (April): 454–479.

———. 1976. *Perception and Misperception in International Politics.* Princeton: Princeton University Press.

———. 1979. Deterrence Theory Revisited. *World Politics* 31 (January): 289–324.

———. 1982–83. Deterrence and Perception. *International Security* 7 (Winter): 3–30.

Jones, F. C. 1954. *Japan's New Order in Asia: Its Rise and Fall, 1937–45.* London: Oxford University Press.

Kahn, David 1973. *The Code Breakers.* London: Sphere Books.

Knorr, Klaus. 1964. Failures in National Intelligence Estimates: The Case of the Cuban Missiles. *World Politics* 24 (April): 455–467.

Kubek, Anthony. 1965. *How the Far East Was Lost.* Chicago: Regnery.

Langer, William L., and Gleason, S. Everett. 1953. *The Undeclared War, 1940–41.* New York: Harper.

Lanir, Zvi. 1981. *Israel's Involvement in Lebanon: A Precedent for an "Open" Game with Syria?* Tel Aviv: Center for Strategic Studies, Paper No. 10.

Lauren, Paul Gordon. 1979. Theories of Bargaining with Threats of Force: Deterrence and Coercive Diplomacy. In Paul Gordon Lauren (ed.), *Diplomacy: New Approaches in History, Theory, and Policy.* New York: Free Press.

Lebow, Richard Ned. 1981. *Between Peace and War: The Nature of International Crisis.* Baltimore: Johns Hopkins University Press.

Leighton, Richard M., and Coakley, Robert W. 1955. *Global Logistics and Strategy, 1940–1943.* Washington, D.C.: U.S. Department of the Army.

Leopold, Richard W. 1962. *The Growth of American Foreign Policy: A History.* New York: Alfred A. Knopf.

Lockhart, Charles. 1977. Problems in the Management and Resolution of International Conflicts. *World Politics* 29 (April): 370–403.

————. 1981. *Bargaining in International Conflicts*. New York: Columbia University Press.

Luard, Evan. 1967. Conciliation and Deterrence: A Comparison of Political Strategies in the Interwar and Postwar Periods. *World Politics* 19 (January): 167–189.

May, Ernest R. 1973a. *"Lessons" of the Past: The Use and Abuse of History in American Foreign Policy*. New York: Oxford University Press.

————. 1973b. U.S. Press Coverage of Japan, 1931–1941. In *Pearl Harbor as History*. See Borg and Okamoto (1973).

McClelland, Charles A. 1962. General Systems and the Social Sciences. *Etc.: A Review of General Semantics* 18 (February): 449–468.

Meskill, Johanna M. 1966. *Hitler and Japan: The Hollow Alliance*. New York: Atherton Press.

Morgan, Patrick M. 1977. *Deterrence: A Conceptual Analysis*. Beverly Hills, Calif.: Sage Publications.

Morgenstern, George. 1947. *Pearl Harbor: The Story of the Secret War*. New York: Devin Adair.

Morgenthau, Henry M., Jr. 1933–1945. *The Morgenthau Diary*. Hyde Park, N.Y.: Franklin D. Roosevelt Library.

————. 1937–1941. *Presidential Diaries*. Hyde Park, N.Y.: Franklin D. Roosevelt Library.

Morison, Elting E. 1948. Did Roosevelt Start the War?: History Through a Beard. *Atlantic Monthly*, August, pp. 91–97.

————. 1960. *Turmoil and Tradition: The Study of the Life and Times of Henry L Stimson*. Boston: Houghton Mifflin.

Morley, James William. 1976. The Tripartite Pact, 1939–1940: An Introduction. In James William Morely (ed.), *Deterrent Diplomacy: Japan, Germany, and the USSR, 1935–1940*. New York: Columbia University Press.

Morton, Louis. 1962. *Strategy and Command, The First Two Years: The War in the Pacific*. Washington, D.C.: U.S. Department of the Army.

Neumann, William L. 1957. Ambiguity and Ambivalence in Ideas of National Interest in Asia. In Alexander DeConde (ed.), *Isolation and Security*. Durham, N.C.: Duke University Press.

————. 1963. *America Encounters Japan, From Perry to MacArthur*. Baltimore: Johns Hopkins University Press.

North, Robert. 1967. Perception and Action in the 1914 Crisis. *Journal of International Affairs* 21: 103–122.

Nixon, Edgar B. 1969. *Franklin D. Roosevelt and Foreign Affairs*. 3 vols. Cambridge: Belknap Press of Harvard University Press.

Osgood, Robert Endicott. 1953. *Ideals and Self-Interest in America's Foreign Relations.* Chicago: University of Chicago Press.

Pelz, Stephen E. 1974. *Race to Pearl Harbor: The Failure of the Second London Naval Conference and the Onset of World War II.* Cambridge: Harvard University Press.

Perkins, Dexter. 1954. Was Roosevelt Wrong? *Virginia Quarterly Review* 30 (Summer): 355–372.

———. 1957. *The New Age of Franklin Roosevelt, 1932–45.* Chicago: University of Chicago Press.

Pipes, Richard. 1981. American Perceptions and Misperceptions of Soviet Military Intentions and Capabilities. In Robert Pfaltzgraff, Jr., Uri Ra'anan, and Warren Milberg (eds.), *Intelligence Policy and National Security.* London: Macmillan.

Pogue, Forrest C. 1966. *George C. Marshall: Ordeal and Hope, 1939–1942.* New York: Viking.

Pratt, Julius. 1964. *Cordell Hull* New York: Cooper Square.

Range, Willard. 1959. *Franklin D. Roosevelt's World Order.* Atlanta: University of Georgia Press.

Rapoport, Anatol. 1960. *Fights, Games, and Debates.* Ann Arbor: University of Michigan Press.

Rappaport, Armin. 1963. *Henry L Stimson and Japan, 1931–33.* Chicago: University of Chicago Press.

Rauch, Basil. 1950. *Roosevelt, From Munich to Pearl Harbor: A Study in the Creation of a Foreign Policy.* New York: Creative Age Press.

Rochester, J. Martin. 1978. The Paradigm Debate in International Relations and Its Implications for Foreign Policy-Making: Toward a Redefinition of the National Interest. *Western Political Quarterly* 31 (March): 48–58.

Roosevelt, Eleanor. 1949. *This I Remember.* New York: Harper.

Roosevelt, Elliot, ed. 1950. *F.D.R.: His Personal Letters, 1928–45.* 3 vols. New York: Duell, Sloan, and Pearce.

Roosevelt, Franklin D. 1933–1945. *Papers as President: President's Official File.* Hyde Park, N.Y.: Franklin D. Roosevelt Library.

———. 1933–1945. *President's Personal File.* Hyde Park, N.Y.: Franklin D. Roosevelt Library.

———. 1933–1945. *President's Secretary's File.* Hyde Park, N.Y.: Franklin D. Roosevelt Library.

———1933–1945. *Press Conferences.* Hyde Park, N.Y.: Franklin D. Roosevelt Library.

Rosenman, Samuel I, ed. 1950. *The Public Papers and Addresses of Franklin D. Roosevelt.* 8 vols. New York: Harper.

Roskin, Michael. 1974. From Pearl Harbor to Vietnam: Shifting Generational Paradigms and Foreign Policy. *Political Science Quarterly* 89 (Fall): 563–588.

Russett, Bruce. 1967. Pearl Harbor: Deterrence Theory and Decision Theory. *Journal of Peace Research* 2: 89–105.

———. 1972. *No Clear and Present Danger: A Skeptical View of the United States' Entry into World War II*. New York: Harper Torchbooks.

Sadao, Ashada. 1973. The Japanese Navy and the United States. In *Pearl Harbor as History*. See Borg and Okamoto (1973).

Sanborn, Frederick R. 1951. *Design for War: A Study of Secret Power Policy, 1933–1941*. Chicago: Regnery.

Schelling, Thomas. 1960. *The Strategy of Conflict*. New York: Oxford University Press.

Schlesinger, Arthur Jr. 1960. *The Age of Roosevelt: The Politics of Upheaval*. Boston: Houghton Mifflin.

———. 1967. Origins of the Cold War. *Foreign Affairs*. 46 (October): 22–52.

Schroeder, Paul W. 1958. *The Axis Alliance and Japanese-American Relations, 1941*. Ithaca: Cornell University Press.

Sherwood, Robert E. 1948. *Roosevelt and Hopkins: An Intimate History*. New York: Harper.

Snyder, Glenn H., and Diesing, Paul. 1977. *Conflict Among Nations: Bargaining, Decision-Making, and System Structure in International Crises* Princeton: Princeton University Press.

Stein, Janice G., and Brecher, Michael. 1976. Image, Advocacy and the Analysis of Conflict: An Israeli Case Study. *Jerusalem Journal of International Relations* 1 (Spring): 33–58.

Steinbrunner, John D. 1974. *The Cybernetic Theory of Decision*. Princeton: Princeton University Press.

Stimson, Henry L. 1930–1945. *Correspondence*. New Haven: Yale University Library.

———. 1930–1945. *Diary*. New Haven: Yale University Library.

———. 1936. *The Far Eastern Crisis: Recollections and Observations*. New York: Harper.

Stimson, Henry L., and Bundy, McGeorge. 1948. *On Active Service in Peace and War*. New York: Harper.

Suedfeld, Peter, and Tetlock, Philip. 1977. Integrative Complexity of Communications in International Crisis. *Journal of Conflict Resolution* 21 (March): 169–184.

Tansill, Charles C. 1952. *Back Door to War: The Roosevelt Foreign Policy, 1933–1941*. Chicago: Regnery.

Thies, Wallace J. 1980. *When Governments Collide.* Berkeley: University of California Press.

Thomson, James C., Jr. 1973. The Role of the Department of State. In *Pearl Harbor as History.* See Borg and Okamoto (1973).

Toland, John. 1970. *The Rising Sun: The Decline and Fall of the Japanese Empire, 1936–1945.* New York: Random House.

Touval, Saadia. 1973. *Domestic Dynamics of Change from Confrontation to Accommodation Policies* (Research Monograph No. 38). Princeton: Center of International Studies, Princeton University.

Tsou, Tang. 1963. *America's Failure in China, 1941–1950.* Chicago: University of Chicago Press.

Tsunoda, Jun. 1980. The Navy's Role in the Southern Strategy. In James William Morley (ed.), *The Fateful Choice: Japan's Advance into Southwest Asia, 1939–1941.* New York: Columbia University Press.

Tuchman, Barbara W. 1970. *Stilwell and the American Experience in China, 1911–1945.* New York: Macmillan.

U.S. Congress Joint Committee on the Investigation of Pearl Harbor Attack. 1946. *Hearings* (79th Congress, 1st Session). Washington, D.C.: U.S. Government Printing Office.

U.S. Department of State. 1941–43. *Foreign Relations of the United States: Diplomatic Papers, the Far East: 1938, 1940, 1941.* Washington, D.C.: U.S. Government Printing Office.

———. 1943. *Papers Relating to the Foreign Relations of the U.S.–Japan: 1931–1941.* 2 vols. Washington, D.C.: U.S. Government Printing Office.

Weigley, Russell F. 1973. The Role of the War Department and the Army. In *Pearl Harbor as History.* See Borg and Okamoto (1973).

Wellborn, Fred W. 1960. *Diplomatic History of the United States.* Totowa, N.J.: Littlefield.

Welles, Sumner. 1944. *The Time for Decision.* New York: Harper.

———. 1950. *Seven Decisions That Shaped History.* New York: Harper.

White, Robert R. 1965. Images in the Context of International Conflict. In Herbert C. Kelman (ed.), *International Behavior: A Social Psychological Analysis.* New York: Holt, Rinehart and Winston.

Wohlstetter, Roberta. 1962. *Pearl Harbor: Warning and Decision.* Stanford, Calif.: Stanford University Press.

Yergin, Daniel. 1977. *Shattered Peace: The Origins of the Cold War and the National Security State.* Boston: Houghton Mifflin.

Young, Oran Y. 1967. *The Intermediaries: Third Parties in International Crises.* Princeton: Princeton University Press.

———. 1968. *The Politics of Force: Bargaining During International Crises.* Princeton: Princeton University Press.

Index